WHY UNIONS MATTER

WHY
UNIONS
MATTER

Michael D. Yates

Monthly Review Press
New York

Cover art courtesy of Eva Fasanella

Library of Congress Cataloging-in-Publication Data

Yates, Michael, 1946-
    Why Unions Matter / Michael D. Yates.
        p.   cm.
    Includes bibliographical references and index.
    ISBN 0-85345-930-4 (hardcover). — ISBN 0-85345-929-0 (pbk.)
    1. Trade-unions—United States. I. Title.
    HD6508.Y38 1998
    331.88'0973—dc21   98-13171
                                                  CIP

Monthly Review Press
122 West 27th Street
New York, NY 10001

Manufactured in the United States of America

10 9 8 7 6 5 4 3 2 1

To my mother, Irene Yates,
for all of her hard work, encouragement, and love.

CONTENTS

LIST OF TABLES

ACKNOWLEDGMENTS

I want to thank Ethan Young at Monthly Review Press for helping to get this book started and for his helpful comments and criticisms along the way. Christopher Phelps's fine editorial skills and attention to detail have been much appreciated. Paul LeBlanc, a fine historian and writer, read the entire manuscript and made many useful comments and corrected some glaring errors and omissions. Historian Priscilla Murolo graciously provided me with an annotated bibliography of books and articles concerning the labor history of women. Louis Proyect, a friend and long-time champion of the working class, made helpful comments and gave generous encouragement. My long-time friends and colleagues, Bruce Williams and Monica Frolander-Ulf, have helped me to think and write about (as well as try to organize) unions. Useful resources were suggested by several members of the Progressive Economists Network (PEN-L): Doug Henwood, Bryan Thompson, Richard Robbins, Ellen Frank, Elaine Bernard, Ellen Dannin, and William Puette. Donald Spatz, Treasurer of Workers' Education Local 189 of the Communications Workers of America, kindly sent me a copy of the local's *Directory of Labor Education,* an indispensable guide to resources for workers. Labor educator and activist Fernando Gapasin provided much useful information on Central Labor Councils and on current labor insurgencies. Special thanks go to Howard Harris for first hiring me as a labor educator; it has been through teaching workers that I learned how to write a book like this.

I am indebted to Paul Sweezy and Harry Magdoff of *Monthly Review* for their friendly and consistent encouragement. Their lives and work are an inspiration to all of us. I am also grateful for the special kindness shown by the late Judy Ruben of Monthly Review Press. Her untimely death has saddened us beyond words. I am pleased to acknowledge, too, the inspiration of the work of *Monthly Review*'s cofounder, the late Leo Huberman. His 1946 pamphlet, *The Truth About Unions*, provided the model for this book, and his work as a labor educator, union activist, and popular writer gave me a model for my own working life.

Finally, I want to thank my partner, Karen Korenoski. Not only has she been a keen critic, but she has also given me the kind of love which makes life worth living.

INTRODUCTION

Meadville, Pennsylvania, is a small town located some one hundred miles north of Pittsburgh. A few miles outside of town there is a factory which manufactures plate glass. It is owned by PPG Industries, a large, profitable conglomerate, one of the glass industry's leaders. When the plant was built, the company was known simply as Pittsburgh Plate Glass, but it took on the more impersonal initials as it diversified. It now employs about 330 production workers in rotating shifts, making plate glass twenty-four hours a day, seven days a week. Most of them are white men, although a significant number of women work the lines as well.

In the fall of 1994 one of the workers telephoned and asked me to speak to his coworkers about their legal rights.[1] They were in the middle of a union organizing drive, and the management was turning up the heat. I said that I could not come unless the union trying to organize the plant approved. A few weeks later he called to say that the union, the Aluminum, Brick, and Glass Workers (ABG), had agreed that I should visit. In a fire hall close to the plant, I spoke twice to about sixty men and women. My talks were videotaped and later circulated around the plant. Six months after my visit, I returned at the request of the national union to speak again, the day before the election. I gave three speeches, one for each shift, to about a hundred workers. Unfortunately our efforts were not quite sufficient to beat the corporation's anti-union campaign. The next day the union was defeated by twenty votes. The union supporters were devastated, but they vowed to try again.

My experiences at the Meadville plant were instructive and emotionally intense. I went to high school with some of the union's strongest supporters; they had moved to Meadville from our hometown, which once boasted the largest glass factory in the world. I had not seen them in thirty years and we had traveled different paths, but we still had much in common. They remembered our town as a union stronghold, a place where working people could make a decent living, where they stuck together, where your identity depended on where you stood, with the company or the union. Although, like myself, they did not know then what the union had meant to their hard-working parents, they knew now. Experience had taught them the hard lesson that when you are unorganized you are at the mercy of the company, and that as a rule, despite pronouncements to the contrary, the company did not show much mercy.

The Meadville plant was one of many built by PPG to defeat the union after the great strike of 1958. The company began to locate glass plants in isolated rural areas with few or no union traditions, especially in the South. New hires were carefully screened so that not too many workers infected with the union spirit were employed. Not too many people from any one town were hired, so that the company could be assured that their workers would not socialize much. Hourly wage rates were close to union rates, and workers could earn more through incentives and bonuses. Sometimes all workers were paid a salary, just like the managers. New methods of personnel management were utilized, including the formation of teams.[2] Team leaders were selected by supervisors for special training, often at hotels with all expenses paid.

Most workplaces are profoundly alienating, and unions can help workers to overcome their isolation. Employers know this, and therefore try to devise company-dominated arrangements which they hope will serve as substitutes for unions. The basic idea is to group the workers into "quality circles," which then brainstorm more efficient ways to work, or into "teams," which serve as problem-solvers for management. Each team member is trained to do every other member's job. Management provides special training for circles and teams, often outside of the workplace and under the supervision of supposedly neutral experts. This training deliberately imparts the impression that the employer is concerned with the workers as human beings with needs beyond the workplace. Employers may even provide special technical training and give workers access to company data so that the teams can, in fact, solve problems and take on some of the work previously done by lower-level management.

Workers, desperate for any kind of attention, often are enthusiastic about teams. But in time most find that management uses teams for one reason only—to increase productivity and profits. Since most jobs have been engineered to require as few real skills as possible, the fact that team members know each other's jobs means that management will not have to hire replacements when a member is sick or injured. Workers may find it more interesting to keep exact track of every move they make on a job, but employers have them do this in order to reduce the amount of labor used. When workers make suggestions for increasing productivity, they are giving to their employer the knowledge which will eventually allow the employer to speed up their work or eliminate their jobs. When jobs are re-evaluated with team assistance, workers may be helping the employer to discover which jobs can be profitably contracted out. When team members are called "associates" instead of workers, the employer is using manipulative psychology to give workers the trappings of power without relinquishing any real control.

The company's anti-union strategy was successful, leaving the union a shell of its former self. To survive, it had to become a catch-all union, organizing anyone it could. It was also forced to merge with other unions; first it merged with a brick and aluminum workers' union, and then with the United Steelworkers of America. Yet despite all that PPG has done to remain union-free, it has not been able to stamp out its employees' yearnings for something better. Nothing has erased the benefits of a union from the memories of my old classmates. At the Meadville plant everyone was an employee "at will." This meant that a worker could be fired or otherwise discriminated against for any reason not protected by a written law. No employee could be discharged for union activity or because of race, sex, religion, ethnicity, national origin, age, or disability. But employees could be fired for *any* other reason: a disagreement with the foreman, an argument with a coworker, a political difference, a refusal to attend a company function, or a failure to perform work which they thought too dangerous. Every year tens of thousands of people are discharged for these and many other reasons.

But if they had been in a union, they could not have been fired except for *just cause*. Every union contract includes a grievance procedure, giving each worker the *right* to file a complaint against the company for any discrimination. Nearly all contracts provide that a neutral person, one not employed by the company, will resolve the dispute if the parties themselves cannot do so. In other words, with a union the employer must have a good reason to fire someone.[3]

While the base wages at Meadville were comparable to those earned at union plants, the fringe benefits were not. At one of our meetings a pensioner spoke. His voice cracking, he told us that after thirty years of hard labor, he now received merely $400 a month. If he died, his wife would get half as much. The company had already reduced his health benefits and was threatening to cut them off altogether. The pensioner implored those at the meeting to vote union. With a union, employer-provided benefits are the employer's contractual obligations. They cannot be changed without the consent of the union. (My father retired from a union PPG plant in 1984, and his pension was nearly twice that of the nonunion pensioner. My father had full health coverage as well, better than that received by the current workers at the nonunion facility.)

Our work lives are full of uncertainty and insecurity. At any time we might find ourselves out in the street without work. In this era of corporate downsizing and plant closing it is a rare worker who has not faced job loss. Workers are often fired or laid off without notice. At the time of the union election, the Meadville plant was about to close one of the tanks in which the glass is made for rebuilding, a project slated to take about a year and a half. The workers "enjoyed" (again at the will of the employer) recall rights for thirteen months after a layoff; after that they would be considered new hires. Many feared that when the tank work was done, they would have no recall rights and would be hired back as temporary or part-time workers. In the union plants employees had unlimited recall rights. Of course, no union can really guarantee employment, but if there is work, its members will get it. If a plant closes, the union members may be able to transfer to another plant with no loss of wages, benefits, or seniority.

During my visits I heard again and again something else that a union would do. It would force the company, so long accustomed to seeing its employees as simply costs of production, to treat workers as human beings, with the respect that all people deserve. In the words of the old labor anthem "Solidarity Forever," the union would "make them strong," literally. I know that many of the people gathered in that fire hall would have voted for the union for this reason alone. In fact, the union organizing drive, in itself, had already made them strong. To show their support for the union, more than one hundred workers wore bright red union t-shirts to work. It took tremendous courage to take this symbolic action, which showed their supervisors that they were no longer just individuals who would meekly do what they were told. The bosses hated these shirts and tried to get the workers to stop wearing them, but this only reinforced the feeling of power which the shirts gave them. The shirts must have made them feel like the auto workers who pulled the stop switches on the assembly lines right before the great sitdown strikes of the 1930s. Observers said that you could feel the power which the workers now knew they had. Of all the things which a union brings, this understanding of workers' power is the most important.

Most people in the United States are workers, although this is difficult to discern from our media, scholarly journals, and popular culture. Somehow all we hear about are the rich, a very broad middle class, and the underclass of poor. Much attention is paid to the poor, who are presumed to be sociopathic and in need of special attention. The middle class includes everyone not in the underclass and not filthy rich: the clerk at Sears is middle class, and so is the doctor and the lawyer. Here is the "silent majority" of solid citizens extolled by our presidents and editorial writers. The rich avoid scrutiny altogether except when one of them does something outrageous or when, through pluck and courage, some former nobody fights his way into their ranks.

This threefold social division obscures what is most important to know, namely that we have a *capitalist* economic system which by its nature divides society into two classes: those who own the workplaces and those who work for them. Ownership is highly unequal. A good 90 percent of the people own nothing, while a fraction of the rest own almost everything.[4] This monopoly of ownership gives the owners a great advantage, namely, that everyone else depends on them to live. That is, we have to sell to them our ability to work, or we will be in serious trouble. It takes no leap of the imagination to realize that, others things equal, we will not get the better of this transaction. We will be subject to the threat of job loss anytime our employers can find cheaper labor or get machines to do our work, or whenever the economy sinks into depression.

The working class majority in the United States has suffered great hardships for the past twenty-five years. The purchasing power of its wages has declined dramatically, as has the purchasing power of its fringe benefits. Millions of workers have lost their health insurance and an increasing proportion of new workers have none to begin with. Those working must work longer hours to make ends meet, and more and more families have to send at least two members into the workforce. More and more workers are "contingent," without full-time status or long-term security. At any given time, at least eight million persons are unemployed. It is no wonder that families are under siege and that society confronts homelessness, violence, and rampant drug abuse, to name a few of our social ills.[5]

Much has been written about the decline of the "middle class," in actuality the decline of the working class. This decline is attributed to a variety of sources: the increasing sophistication of technology and the inability of most people to understand it (in turn, the fault of our public schools); the loss of a work ethic due mainly to the generosity of the welfare state; high taxes; overpopulation (especially if the focus is international); foreign aid; and savage foreign competition.[6]

One issue is almost always missing from these analyses: *class power.* The decline in working class living standards corresponds closely with the decimation of the primary defender of workers: the labor union. In a society structured like ours, it is impossible for any given individual to safeguard his economic position. Only by acting together, in union, can most of us hope to face the owners of the nation's vast wealth with anything approaching a level playing field. Somehow this has become a great secret in this country, but it is easily proven that when workers are organized in unions they are demonstrably better off than when they are not.

This book will argue that no amount of education and training, no cut in taxes, and no rise in productivity can do for workers what their unionization can achieve. In this book we will explore what unions are, how they work, what they do, and why they improve the lives of their members. We will learn the difference unions make, both in terms of overall statistics and individual case studies. We will become familiar with important aspects of trade union activity: picketing, strikes, and corporate campaigns, as well as shop stewards, grievances, arbitration, and collective bargaining.

This book's picture of unions is positive, but it does not obscure grave difficulties. A majority of the workers at the Meadville glass factory did, after all, vote against the union. Given the overwhelming benefits of unionization, why did they do this? If unions are so good, why do so few Americans belong to them? In examining the reasons for low and declining union density in the United States, this book will make a distinction between reasons external to the labor movement and those internal to it. With respect to external obstacles, we will look at the anti-labor bias of the laws, the exceptionally close alliance between business and the government, and the deep animosity of the media toward organized labor. With respect to internal failings of trade unions, we will direct our attention to the failure to aggressively organize new members; racism, sexism, and corruption in the labor movement; the need for consistent union democracy; and the lack of an independent labor politics.

How can unions regain their former strength and increase it? The most important idea developed here is that unions can only grow when they are a part of a larger social and political movement. However, a working class social movement can best be built with unions as one of its primary components. Therefore, the growth of unions and the development of a wider movement for social change must occur together, and we will describe concrete steps which can be taken to make both events a reality.

CHAPTER ONE

WHY UNIONS?

Let's be honest. Almost every person who works for a living works for someone else. We work in all sorts of jobs, in all types of industries, and under all kinds of conditions. But no matter what the exact circumstances, we do not work for ourselves or for each other, which means that the most fundamental aspects of our work are not controlled by us. Furthermore, our employers try to organize their workplaces so that we cannot exert much control by our own actions. For example, each of us needs to work; we do not labor for the fun of it but to pay our bills and support our families. Yet none of us can guarantee that we will have work on any given day, let alone for an entire working life. If our employer decides to shut down the business, move it, or introduce labor-saving machinery, none of us acting alone can do anything about it.

I am a college teacher, and I have been working for the same school for twenty-nine years. By most accounts I am a good teacher; I once even won an award for my teaching. Most people would say that my job requires a lot of skill; I certainly had to be a student for a long time to qualify to do it. Suppose that I believe that I am being paid too little for my work. I go to my supervisor, and I tell him this. He is sympathetic and says that he will see what he can do. Weeks go by and nothing happens, so I go back to his office. He tells me that he would like to give me more money, but the budget for the school is tight and there is nothing he can do now. If at this point, I tell him that I cannot work for the money I am being paid and that I will have to seek other employment at the end of the school year, what do you suppose he will say? Will my threat

Auto assembler at Chrysler's Jefferson North plant, Detroit, 1994. (Jim West)

to leave get me more money? I doubt it. He will know that if I do leave, the college will do one of two things. It may place advertisements for my replacement, and at least one hundred applicants will seek my job. They will all work for less than my salary, and the college will be under no obligation to grant them the type of job security which I now have. Or, the college will not replace me at all, and will simply eliminate my classes, assign them to the remaining teachers, or hire part-timers to teach some of them. In other words, I am replaceable, and nothing I can do myself can change this. When push comes to shove, my employer holds all of the cards.

What is true for me is true for the overwhelming majority of workers. If you do not believe me, just ask yourself what your boss would say if you insisted on a significant raise and said that you would not work without one. Naturally you do not have to confine yourself to a pay hike. Try insisting that your hours must be cut with no loss of wages, or that your employer must finance a pension for you, or that you must have expensive safety equipment to do your job without risking your health, or that your buddy who was fired be reinstated. You can ask for all of these things, but you cannot force the employer to give them to you by your own actions.

If we are honest, we must admit that our employers have real power over us. Some of them may be nice and some of them may be nasty, but none of them will spend money just because it would be good for one of us. They know that as individuals we are less powerful than they are. We have only our ability to work to sell, but they have the jobs. In our economic system, these jobs belong to them and not to us, and they can do with them whatever they want. It is a simple but powerful truth that working people and their employers do not face each other as equals. Their employers have the jobs they need, and workers are replaceable.[1]

STRENGTH IN NUMBERS

While most working people know that they cannot do much on their own, some choose to ignore this fact. Perhaps they are afraid, or maybe they believe that they will become supervisors some day, or maybe they think that they deserve to be controlled by someone else. Sooner or later, however, most workers will draw the obvious conclusion: if they stick together with their fellow workers, they can change things. Usually something will happen at work that sparks general anger and resentment. My wife and my daughter once worked at a daycare center run by a large national corporation. Despite the pitifully low pay, most of the women there enjoyed working with young children, and most of them showed very little day-to-day animosity toward their employer. Yet they were unhappy about nearly every aspect of their work. Once a month the supervisor had an after-work staff meeting to inform the workers of changes in policies and to give them the impression that management was concerned about employee welfare. Ordinarily, none of them had the nerve to openly challenge the office manager at one of these meetings, despite the fact that most of them couldn't stand her personally and had the deepest dislike for the company. Right before one meeting, the company issued a directive that each worker had to wear a uniform and a name tag. This led to a lot of grumbling and discussion. A few people said that they would not comply with this policy, and if they were forced to, they would quit. At the meeting, my wife brought the issue out in the open, along with other complaints, including direct criticisms of the manager. Her courage stiffened the backbones of others, and before long, a barrage of angry comments filled the

(Mike Konopacki)

air. Faced with such a revolt the supervisor was forced to retreat and make promises that she would investigate some of the complaints. And no one wore a uniform!

Direct actions such as this occur every day in thousands of workplaces around the world. Through them workers learn the power of solidarity and begin to understand the great gap between what is and what could be. At the daycare center "what is" is the minimum wage, few benefits, onerous working conditions, favoritism, and no respect.[2] But this is certainly not "what could be." Surely those who care for our children deserve much better, but the corporation's greed and the inability of the workers to exert their collective power prevent "what could be" from becoming reality.

After the meeting, a few of the women began to discuss their work situation more seriously. Out of these discussions, they came up with a plan of action, based upon their knowledge that the center's contract to provide daycare was about to expire. The daycare provider is under contract with a large university hospital, and many of the children's parents work for the hospital. A contingent of daycare workers went to see the hospital administrator who deals regularly with the provider, and workers also began to speak with sympathetic parents. Their message was that unless the hospital chose a new provider, they would quit the center. This was especially upsetting to the parents, whose children were quite attached to the workers, and who frequently had to hire sitters to care for their children at home in evenings and on weekends. The hospital also did not want a mass exodus of skilled and caring workers. Ultimately the company's contract was not renewed, and a new provider was chosen, paying higher wages and offering better benefits. On the other hand, not all of the workers have been hired by the new center.

While the spontaneous organizing just described occurs all of the time and often results in gains for the workers, it is not enough to insure permanent results. First, workers quit, retire, and move, so the workers who win a particular struggle may not be there for the next fight. Second, workers may not always have the energy for direct actions, especially in situations which they may not perceive as very important. For example, suppose a worker is fired unfairly, but he has a spotty work record and is not universally loved by his coworkers. It is unlikely that they will threaten to quit unless he is reinstated. Third, long-term improvement in the conditions of employment may require money and constant attention. Thus, it is not surprising that working people have come to the realization that more formal organizing is necessary. In all capitalist societies, those who toil for others have formed *labor unions* to defend themselves and advance their interests in the face of powerful employers.[3]

In many ways a labor union is like any other voluntary organization. Say some residents in a community are unhappy with the condition of their streets, schools, and playgrounds. Some activists call a meeting at a local church, and a large number of people show up. After they voice their concerns, someone proposes that they form a neighborhood association to pressure the town's leaders to do something about their problems. Some temporary officers are elected, and regular meetings are established. Plans of action are formulated, and tactics for achieving the groups' goals are worked out. A committee is formed to devise a set of bylaws for the organization, and these include provisions for the selection of officers, outlining the purpose of the organization, conditions of membership, and so forth. As the group grows and achieves some successes, its members decide to assess dues on members, rent office space, obtain some used office equipment, and hire an office manager. The more or less spontaneous actions which led to the original formation have generated a more formal, structured, and hopefully permanent institution.[4]

What distinguishes labor unions from other voluntary organizations is that they are formed in response to the daily grind of working for others. The understanding that workers, as individuals, are powerless leads toward recognition that they share this powerlessness with others. They begin to identify with their workmates, and this identification, based upon shared work experience, is the root cause of the formation of a labor union. When this sense of identity as working people combines with enough frustration at work, actions follow: spontaneous walkouts or slowdowns, forced meetings with the bosses, the stopping of the work process. Sooner or later, the need for a permanent defender, an independent organization standing ready to take on the employer, is felt—and the labor union is born.

THE FIRST U.S. UNIONS[5]

In 1776 there were not very many wage laborers in the United States. Most workers in the South were, of course, slaves. In the North, most people were farmers. What little manufacturing existed was carried on in small shops organized on a guild model, with young apprentices learning a trade taught them by skilled journeymen and master craftsmen. The masters owned the shops, but they worked alongside their men, most of whom aspired to become masters themselves. With the onset of the nineteenth century, however, things began to change dramatically. The possibility of making large sums of money grew with the development of mass markets for items like shoes and clothing. Masters began to see that if they organized their shops in a more hierarchical way, they could increase their profits. They began to take on more apprentices, but they confined them to doing unskilled work. And they began to resist any demands by their journeymen (skilled manufacturing workers) for higher "prices" for their work— that is, more pay. At the same time, the invention of labor-saving and skill-reducing machines such as power looms led to the construction of factories in which large quantities of goods could be produced. These factories, especially the textile mills of New England, began to hire young farm girls to do the work. In these factories, there was a clear separation between the workers and the owners from the beginning, whereas in the small craft shops, it took the journeymen some time to see that their interests were separate from those of the masters.

As the differences between workers and owners sharpened and became clearer, the journeymen did what workers always do. They began to organize to protect themselves. In Philadelphia in 1806, shoemakers (or cordwainers as they were then called) presented the city's shoe masters with a "price list" for the various types of work they did. When the masters refused to honor their list, the cordwainers said that they would not work for any master who would not pay them their prices. And they would not work alongside of any cordwainer who would work for less than the proposed rates. What they were trying to do was to create a "closed shop," that is, an arrangement in which the masters could not hire anyone who was not a member of the journeymen's union. Likewise, the young women in the textile factories struck to protest wage cuts. A strike in Lowell, Massachusetts, in 1834 encompassed one-sixth of the city's entire workforce.[6]

These early attempts at unionization met with a host of obstacles. The economy was subject to sudden depressions, and the unemployment which resulted quickly destroyed the unions. The employers aggressively resisted the efforts of their upstart workers, and the press and many politicians condemned the unions as threats to liberty. The Philadelphia cordwainers were taken to court by the masters, and the judge ruled that their union was a "criminal conspiracy," worthy of fines and jail time for the members. The law was uniformly hostile to any attempts by workers to organize.[7] Women workers faced special difficulties in organizing. Not only did they have to contend with the normal greed of their employers, but they also had to confront the hostility of men, including most male workers, toward any acts of female independence. As one woman put it, "It needs no small share of courage for us, who have been used to impositions and oppression from our youth up to the present day, to come before the public in defense of our own rights."[8]

Yet workers persevered, moving forward in good times and backward in bad, but always creating the memory for their heirs that only collective actions could improve their lot in life. By the middle of the 1880s, skilled workers, at least, had finally managed to achieve a permanent organization, the American Federation of Labor or AFL.[9]

DO UNIONS WORK?

We are regularly told by employers and by the media that unions are neither necessary nor beneficial for workers. When employers get wind of any attempt by their employees to unionize, they begin a disinformation campaign. They say that workers are no better off with a union than without one, and most likely worse off. Unions, they charge, are undemocratic outsiders whose leaders are interested only in their own power and in filling the union's treasury. They ask workers a simple question: why should they vote in a union when the only "benefit" they will get will be the privilege of paying dues? By their argument, a union will inevitably lead them out on strike, forcing them to lose their paychecks, with no guarantee of any gains; these strikes tend to be violent, and their only result will be the complete breakdown of workplace harmony. Here is part of an actual letter sent by management to some restaurant workers trying to form a union:

> Dear Fellow Employees:
> As you know, there will be a Union election on July 9. At that election each of you will have the opportunity to vote to determine whether or not you want to be represented by the restaurant workers' union.
> You are much luckier than the employees at Fiorello's, our restaurant on the west side. Some time ago those employees voted to be represented by the restaurant workers' union. They were led down the primrose path by Union promises of increased wage benefits. In fact, after the Union negotiated a contract with the restaurant management which, in my opinion, gave the employees at Fiorello's no more than they would have gotten had there been no union—and probably gave them less. In addition, I believe that many of these employees will be hurt by the inflexibility of the Union contract. . . .
> On the other hand, you know from the experience of Fiorello's employees exactly the kind of contract the Union would negotiate if it became your collective bargaining representative. A contract which produces nothing more than you would expect to receive were there no union in the picture. For that, you are afforded the privilege of paying Union dues. . . .
> The restaurant does not want a Union at Fiorello's! Our experience on the west side has shown that we can negotiate an agreement with the Union which does not cost us any more in wages and benefits than without the Union and may even cost less. But our experience on the west side has also shown us that the presence of the Union results in a tense working relationship with extreme disharmony among the employees.
> This is a real cost to everyone. It can result in a loss of customers and a loss of income to our employees who serve those customers, as well as the restaurant itself. The Union benefits no one but itself.[10]

The media seldom present unions in a favorable light, ignoring all of their positive features and highlighting and exaggerating the negative ones. Strike violence always makes the front page, although it is seldom mentioned that employers nearly always instigate such violence.[11] If employers hire scabs to replace the strikers, the media will never question whether the companies should have the right to do so. Instead they will focus attention upon the confrontations between the strikers and the police brought in to insure that the scabs can get through the picket lines. The daily work of unions in securing higher wages and benefits, safer workplaces, and the right to a fair hearing for complaints against the employer is ignored completely. In the more artistic media, such as films, the collective struggles of working people rarely take center stage, and when they do, they tend to be tainted with violence and corruption. Try to remember a popular movie which shows unions in a favorable light. The only one that comes immediately to mind is *Norma Rae*, the exception which proves the rule.[12]

I mention the negative, and, as I shall show, false, popular image of unions for two reasons. First, workers need to be aware of the lies employers will tell them when they attempt to act in their own interests. Second, we must understand that the very nature of our society is disguised and hidden by elaborate propaganda which is repeated so often that most of us have come to think that it is true.[13] It is only a slight exaggeration to state that whatever is good for working people will be presented to us as bad, in newspapers, on radio and television, in the movies, and on the talk shows. Nowhere is this more the case than with unions, and the reason is not hard to discover. The corporate pursuit of profits is the underpinning of our social order, from the daily newspapers to the halls of Congress. Maximum profits require maximum corporate control of our workplaces, which, in turn, means that our employers must be free to control us. Anything which interferes with this control will be portrayed as evil, not just to the employers but to the social order itself. Since a union tries to win some control for us over our lives at work, it provides a direct threat to management. Therefore, unions will be portrayed as evil incarnate, as viruses which must be stamped out for the good of society. The fact that unions are *good* for workers makes the attack upon them all the more important.

TABLE I

Union Wage and Benefit Advantages, 1995

	Wages	Insurance	Pension	Compensation
All Workers				
Union	$16.69	$2.24	$1.15	$22.40
Nonunion	13.35	0.98	0.42	16.26
Union Advantage				
Dollars	$ 3.34	$1.26	$0.73	$6.14
By percent	25	128	174	38
Blue Collar				
Union	$16.81	$2.34	$1.31	$23.07
Nonunion	11.21	0.94	0.31	14.14
Union Advantage				
Dollars	$ 5.60	$1.40	$1.00	$ 8.93
By percent	50	149	323	63

One way to show the union advantage is simply to compare the wages and benefits of union members with those who are not in unions. Table 1 gives us the basic data.[14] In addition to wages, the table also compares differences in two important benefits—insurance (including health insurance) and pensions. Given the insecurities of working life, these are probably the most important benefits, since they protect workers against the ravages of sickness and old age.

Three things should be noted about this data. First, the benefits are given in terms of their wage per hour equivalent; the overall union advantage for pensions, for example, is equal to an additional seventy-three cents per hour. Second, the compensation advantage, which includes the benefits, is greater than the wage advantage. This is because union members enjoy both more and better fringe benefits than do nonunion workers.[15] Third, the union advantage is greater for blue collar workers than for all workers, reflecting the fact that unions are of most benefit to workers of lower status.[16]

Table 1 shows what we might call the "gross" union advantage. We cannot know from these data alone whether the differences between the wages and benefits of union and nonunion workers are due exclusively, or even primarily, to the fact that one group of workers belongs to unions. There may be other characteristics of the workers that would cause their wages to be unequal. For example, workers with more education and greater experience ordinarily earn more money, so some of the difference might be due to the fact that union workers have more education and experience. To take this possibility into account, we have to hold all of the other wage-determining factors (that is, all of them except the workers' union status) constant. In this way, we would be comparing two groups of workers that are alike in all respects except union status. Fortunately, economists use a technique which allows them to do this, and, while it will not prove without *any* doubt that union wages and benefits are higher, it will go a long way toward making the case.

In table 2, the union wage advantage (excluding the benefit advantage) is presented for a variety of employee groups.[17] The following variables which might influence wages besides union status are held constant: years of schooling, potential years of experience, marital status, race, gender, part-time status, whether the worker is in a large metropolitan area, whether the worker is a public employee, the region of the country in which the worker lives, the worker's industry, and the worker's occupation.

While the effect of unionization (with all other variables held constant) varies from group to group, it is always significantly positive. For example, union construction workers earn wages 30 percent higher than do nonunion construction workers, even after we have accounted for all of the other factors which might make the union wages higher. The small effect in "Finance, Insurance, and Real Estate" probably reflects the very low rate of unionization in this industry, while that for "Public Administration" reflects the large number of workers who had relatively high wages before unionization, as well as the fact that wages in federal government employment are not set by collective bargaining.

UNIONS AND DIGNITY

That unions definitely improve the wages and benefits of workers is an important thing to know, since it directly contradicts the anti-union propaganda with which we are more familiar. It also shows that there is nothing sacred about the almighty market. Workers make low wages not because the market dictates that this be so but because they are not powerful enough to make their employers

TABLE 2

Sectoral Breakdown of Union Wage Advantage, 1995

Employee Group	Union Advantage (by percent)
All Wage and Salary Workers	16.7
Private Sector Workers	9.1
Public Sector Workers	2.7
Male Workers	6.6
Female Workers	5.5
White Workers	6.9
Black Workers	6.1
Industry Group	
Construction	30.0
Mining	16.6
Manufacturing	16.4
Transportation, Communications, Utilities	20.5
Wholesale and Retail Trade	5.0
Finance, Insurance, and Real Estate	4.3
Services	3.9
Public Administration	6.4

pay them more. Companies often pay low wages to their U.S. workers, but pay similar workers much higher wages in their European operations. They are compelled to do this because the European workers are either organized or subject to generous minimum wage laws secured by the labor movement.[18]

In a society in which access to money is a life-or-death matter, the fact that unions bring workers more of it is obviously important. However, unions do much more. One of the peculiar features of our economic system is that most of us must sell our ability to work in order to live. When our employers buy this ability, they think of it as their private property, and as with the rest of their property, they think that they have the absolute right to do with it as they see fit. In other words, to them, we are just "costs of production" to be minimized, and our ability to work will be treated no better than the tools and machines—and to the extent that we are easy to replace, probably worse. The nature of our society allows our employers to "objectify" us, to treat us as objects or mere means to the end of making money. Yet we do not think of ourselves in this way. Our ability to work cannot be separated from us, and we are real, live human beings, with a multitude of memories, hopes, and aspirations. Our awareness of ourselves as living beings inevitably comes into conflict with our employers' view of us as mere objects. We want to be treated with dignity and respect, but whether we are or not is a matter of chance, depending upon whether or not our particular employer is a decent person. And even if bosses are decent, they will not and cannot hesitate to sacrifice us for the good of the company.

A fundamental goal of a union is to change the relationship between labor and management. Again and again, when workers are asked why they support the union or what the union has meant to them, they say that their fight for a union was a fight for dignity and respect. Automobile workers in the 1930s said that the supervisors would call them by their badge numbers, not their names.[19] A worker in a company which manufactures chain links says that the boss would just whistle for them.[20] Legally, without a union, workers are "at-will"; they can be discharged, demoted, or transferred for any reason other than those privileged by laws, such as race, sex, disability, and union activity. Our employers are free to treat us as they please, even to cut our wages and eliminate our benefits. A union can, and usually does, change all of this. Union members can take action against their employer whenever the boss shows disrespect for them. They can do this through the grievance procedure of the collective bargaining agreement, and, in addition, the union may stand ready to take direct action on behalf of any of its members.

In scholarly language, what a union does is give workers a "voice" in their workplaces, a way to put themselves on a more equal footing with their employers.[21] Here are two examples. I once worked for two summers in a glass factory. My "office" was in the plant's fire hall. During the first shift the firemen were on call, so they spent most of the day waiting for trouble, drinking coffee and shooting the breeze. Every morning the local union's officers would stop by for a coffee and trade stories about work and the union with the firemen, who might then relay them throughout the plant when they made their safety inspection rounds. The union president was a feisty old-timer with one arm.

Taking a phone order at Domino's Pizza, Detroit, 1997. (Jim West)

He had gotten his arm caught in a grinding machine, and the legend had it that he had had the arm amputated on the spot. He would daily regale us with stories of confrontations with the company and how he had stood up to the plant manager. Even if his tales were a bit exaggerated, what if there had been no union when he had lost his arm? He would have been thrown onto the industrial scrap heap to fend for himself as best he could. But the union contract allowed him to take a job as a gate guard, a job without any great physical demands. He used this job as the base from which he built support for himself as a union leader; everyone who passed through the gate knew him, and he had a lot of time to think and to plan. He had dignity despite his lack of an arm, and he owed this to the union. So too did all of the men and women who had their breath stolen from them by emphysema, one of the consequences of working in a glass factory. Some jobs involved lighter duties, and these were allocated by seniority and not by company decree.

The fate of another worker again shows the union advantage in terms beyond dollars and cents. I was the arbitrator in a case in which a man had been unemployed for two years before finally getting a job with the local water company. The employer had a policy which required the workers to wear shoes with steel toes. It also had agreed to reimburse the employees for shoe purchases up to an amount of $50.00. The man was too poor to buy the shoes, so his grandmother bought them for him. He took the receipt to the company, expecting to get the $50.00, since the shoes had cost more than this. Without warning, his supervisor called him in to his office and accused him of doctoring the receipt, saying that the company knew that the shoes were priced at only $37.95. In other words, he was accused of stealing $12.05 from the company. At the meeting, the worker, flustered because he did not want the employer to know that his grandmother had purchased the shoes, lied and said that he had himself purchased them for the amount shown on the receipt. At this point the worker was fired for theft.

Without a union, the matter would have ended right there, because the company could have discharged him for no reason at all. But as a union member, he had rights which the employer had to respect. The collective bargaining agreement stated that no one in the bargaining unit could be discharged except for "just cause." He filed a *grievance* against the company, demanding his reinstatement with full back pay. The grievance procedure contained a series of steps at which the union and the company could try to resolve the dispute. The employer was out to make an example of this worker, because as it turned out, he had become a solid union member and recently had been elected the *shop steward*, the first-level union representative inside of the plant. He had been aggressively pursuing grievances, trying to make the union stronger by showing the members that it would stand up for them. This is the type of person a company hates, so it decided to fire him, expecting that his short tenure and his lie at the meeting would be enough to convict him.

But the employer was wrong. When the two sides failed to settle his grievance, the union invoked the *arbitration* clause of the agreement, which forced the employer to place the case before a neutral outsider called an *arbitrator*. At the arbitration hearing, the company's attorney tried to bully the union's witnesses and the arbitrator as well. But he could not prove that the employee had altered the receipt. So I, as the arbitrator, ordered the worker back to work with no loss of pay, benefits, or seniority. The employer then took a sentence from my award and used it as the basis for firing the worker a second time. But it fared no better before a second arbitrator or before the state court to which it appealed both awards. After collecting the large back pay due him, the worker resumed his duties as shop steward, a position he still holds today.

A worker standing alone is a worker in trouble. For every Michael Jordan, whose amazing talent gives him tremendous power, there are millions of the rest of us, eminently replaceable. Our only hope is to stand together, and, as we have seen, when we do, we can greatly improve our lots in life. There is no doubt that unions force employers to pay their workers higher wages and to provide them with more and better fringe benefits. And furthermore, unions compel employers to listen to their employees and to respect them as human beings. Employers know these things, and this is why they fight our collective efforts so viciously and spread lies about them. In their disinformation campaigns they have allies in the highest places: in Congress, in the White House, in the corporate-owned media, and in the universities. As we examine labor unions further in the following chapters, it is important that we always remember this: if unions are just in it for themselves, how do we explain their known benefits and why are most employers in an all-out war against them?

CHAPTER TWO

HOW UNIONS FORM

Up until the end of the 1930s, the formation of a union was mainly a contest of power. Employers were intent on keeping their workplaces union-free, and they took whatever steps were necessary, no matter how ruthless. Acts of anti-union violence were common and, though illegal, were seldom punished. In fact, public authorities were often complicit in corporate violence against working people. In the coal towns of Pennsylvania, for example, the notorious coal and iron police hired by the companies to intimidate the miners and their families were actually sanctioned by the state legislature. Union supporters could be fired and blacklisted legally. Employers were free to coerce their workers into signing "yellow dog" contracts in which they promised not to join a union. These were legally enforceable contracts, and union organizers risked fine and imprisonment if they tried to get workers to break these agreements by joining a union. The courts took a dim view of labor organizations and readily issued court orders called *injunctions* forbidding workers to strike, picket, and boycott. More than a thousand of these injunctions were issued in the 1920s alone.[1]

Yet despite the combined forces of the corporations and the government, workers did manage to organize to protect their interests and improve their circumstances. The living conditions of unskilled workers, including most African Americans, were too harsh to allow for much success in forming unions, but skilled workers were sometimes able to overcome the employers' antagonism. They did this through what came to be called *direct actions*. For example, iron molders might force their employer to give in to their collective demands by striking and enforcing their strike with pickets. The molders would typically be white men of the same nationality and with strong community ties. No one would cross their picket lines, and occasionally the local police would not do the employers' bidding. A strike by one group of workers might spread to other groups, who would strike in sympathy. Workers came to understand that the more they stuck together, the better were their chances.[2] A powerful tool of the skilled workers was the *boycott*, asking consumers not to buy products from particular companies charged with unfairness to labor.[3] During the 1880s, thousands of boycotts were called and honored, helping workers to bring recalcitrant employers into line under threat of losing all of their business. Once organized, workers could maintain the union wage scales and conditions only so long as they were prepared to use direct action against their employers any time the employers refused to honor their agreements with the union.

Skilled workers extended their organizations in several ways. First, as their employers began to expand from local to national markets, local unions in different cities and towns banded together to form national unions. One of these that has stood the test of time is the United Mine Workers of America, founded in 1890. Not only was it one of the first successful unions of unskilled and skilled workers, but it was also one of the few unions which actively organized African Americans.[4]

Second, all of the unions in a city began to form central labor bodies or *councils*. Through these local umbrella organizations, unions could coordinate their boycotts and sympathy strikes, as well as labor political activities.

Third, the various unions of skilled workers attempted to build a federation of all national unions. Such a federation could publish a national labor newspaper, act as an arbiter in disputes between national unions, lobby for political reforms, develop a staff of experts on labor affairs, and directly organize new workers into unions, making labor a force to be reckoned with on the national scene. After several attempts, the national unions succeeded in creating the American Federation of Labor (AFL) in 1886, and this federation of many national unions has survived to the present day.

(Mike Konopacki)

Fourth, unions at all levels saw clearly the need for a political response to the alliance which developed between the government and business. It might prove impossible to expand organization if the police and the courts and the legislatures stood ready to stifle labor at every turn. Workers groped for the most appropriate political response, and there was much disagreement. Some argued for the formation of a labor party: a party of, for, and by workers, on the model of the huge labor parties in Europe. Others argued that the situation in the United States made such a party doomed to fail because the two major parties were just too powerful to be challenged. The best political response for labor, they said, was to fight for labor-oriented candidates and policies within the major parties. As the first president of the AFL, the English-born cigar maker Samuel Gompers, put it, labor should "reward its friends and punish its enemies" regardless of their political affiliations. As it turned out, this second argument won the day. It is still the position of organized labor, although the party with which labor is most closely allied is the Democratic Party. But the discussion about labor and politics, and how the alliance of labor and the Democratic Party has failed to promote the interests of workers, is far from finished.[5]

A LITTLE HISTORY

In the decades after the Civil War, which ended in 1865, our economy took on its modern form, one dominated by large corporations. As the opportunities diminished for people to own land for farming or to gain economic independence through owning small businesses, most people were forced to become wage workers. This made them vulnerable to the vagaries of the business cycle— the periodic ups and downs in economic activities characteristic of economies like ours. Over and over, vicious competition among the corporations led them to expand their production too much; they produced more than they could sell. This led to price wars and falling profits, which, in turn, led to massive layoffs and unemployment. The resulting depressions sometimes lasted for many years. During such periods it was difficult for workers to build their unions, because the competition among workers for jobs was too severe. People desperate for work would take the jobs of others if they had to. However, as hard times continued, workers sometimes became so angry at their circumstances that they revolted.

The first worker revolt occurred in 1877, the year of "The Great Uprising."[6] The railroad companies were the nation's largest employers, and among the most ruthless. The economy had been in depression since 1873, and the railroad companies had responded to the crisis by repeatedly cutting the wages of their hard-pressed workers. When the B&O Railroad cut wages by 10 percent in July 1877, workers at its yards in Martinsburg, West Virginia, walked off their jobs in a spontaneous strike. President Rutherford B. Hayes sent in federal troops to stop the strike. But this so angered workers that the strike spread north and west, eventually becoming a national "insurrection." Pittsburgh railroad workers struck the Pennsylvania Railroad on July 19, 1877, and when local militia could not stop the strike, the state government ordered the Philadelphia militia into the city. Hostile crowds met the soldiers. When rocks were thrown, the militiamen opened fire and killed twenty people, including one woman and three children. In response, the workers revolted and destroyed the railroad's property. Order was restored by the workers themselves, although they were defeated later by federal troops. Similar events took place throughout the country, from Chicago to St. Louis to San Francisco. When the strikes were finally crushed, the nation's newspapers condemned the strikers as thugs, tramps, and communists. Citizens were urged to buy guns to protect themselves from the working class rabble.

Other rebellions arose after this first "Uprising," most notably in 1886, 1892, 1894, 1919, and during the Great Depression of the 1930s. In 1886, workers throughout the country struck, boycotted, picketed, and marched to win the eight-hour day. During a rally for the eight-hour day in Haymarket Square in Chicago, a bomb was thrown, perhaps by a police agent, which killed eight policemen.[7] The Chicago police reacted violently, killing a number of workers and wounding scores more. Eight radical labor leaders were arrested soon afterward and charged with murder. Without evidence that they had committed any crime, they were quickly tried and sentenced to death. Four of the eight were hung, and one committed suicide in jail. The others were later pardoned by Governor John Altgeld, whose political career was ruined by this act of mercy. 1894 was the year of the great Homestead steel strike.[8] War broke out in Homestead, Pennsylvania, when steel magnate Andrew Carnegie and his lieutenant Henry Clay Frick shut down the Carnegie Steel Works and then tried to reopen it with nonunion labor. Workers actually took over the government of the town, fighting a pitched battle against a private army of Pinkerton detectives and forcing them to surrender. The strike was only defeated when government troops were brought in. Two years later the Pullman strike erupted. This strike, led by working class hero Eugene V. Debs, began when the workers in the company town of Pullman, Illinois, home of the factory which made the Pullman railroad cars, struck over repeated wage cuts. This monumental battle between employers and workers was again broken by federal troops and court injunctions. Debs was actually sent to prison after the strike for not obeying the injunctions.[9] After the First World War, a massive strike wave, notably in steel, shook the American economy. Historian Philip S. Foner called the 1919 wave "an unprecedented series of uprisings which, if only temporarily, vigorously challenged employers' control of the work force."[10]

There were so many rebellions during the 1930s that it is not possible to examine them all here.[11] In the famous sit-down strikes to organize the unskilled workers in our mass production industries, workers would literally sit down in industrial workplaces, refusing to work or leave. The unemployed took to the streets as well. A strike on the San Francisco docks spread to all workplaces in the city in a general strike in 1934. In Minneapolis, truck drivers led a similar strike, complete with roving bands of picketers and sophisticated logistics.[12] More than one hundred thousand people demonstrated in Chicago in 1932 to protest the murder of several people by police who were trying to enforce an eviction of a family from their home. While police and troops again intervened on the side of the employers, the rebellions of the 1930s could not be defeated. Workers consolidated their unions and were able to win significant political victories.

Apart from a short-lived postwar upheaval in 1945 to 1946, there have been no great labor upheavals since the 1930s. There are two major reasons for this. First, workers have not been able to overcome serious racial and sexual divisions. With some notable exceptions, the labor movement has been dominated by white men, who have often acted in racist and sexist ways, even during the labor rebellions. During the 1930s genuine gains were made in and through many unions against racism and sexism, but after the Second World War organized labor failed to live up to a cherished principle in earlier times: "an injury to one is an injury to all." This meant that the great revolts against racism and sexism of the postwar period, the civil rights movement and the women's movement, were not intimately connected with the labor movement, despite the fact that women and people of color were becoming increasingly important in the workforce.[13] Second, all of the labor rebellions were motivated by a search for alternatives to the wage labor system itself, which many workers could see was the source of their bondage to employers. The challenge to wage labor was part of the politics of the labor movement and the basis for the formation of labor political parties. In the 1930s, conditions were right for forming a labor party and renewing labor's historic antagonism to the system of wage labor. Unfortunately, labor's leaders instead accepted the class structure of American society, allied themselves with the Democratic Party, and eventually purged the left-wing unionists from the labor movement. The result was a more conservative trade unionism, which saw itself more as partner than opponent of employers. So, while there have been many strikes and other militant labor actions since the Great Depression, there has not been a widespread labor rebellion.

HOW UNIONS FORM

The direct action tactics used by skilled workers in the nineteenth century were also used by unskilled workers during the Great Depression of the 1930s. However, the depth of the economic crisis combined with the breadth of the labor movement helped to secure for working people significant political concessions. Renewed militance led to the formation of a new national federation of unions, the Congress of Industrial Organization (CIO). Feeling the pressure from below, the federal government under Franklin D. Roosevelt passed laws which, for the first time, gave workers certain fundamental rights.[14] The Norris-LaGuardia Act of 1932 strictly limited the ability of employers to obtain injunctions in labor disputes. The Fair Labor Standards Act of 1937 provided for the payment of a minimum wage and overtime pay for hours in excess of forty per week. These laws represented major victories for workers, but the most important law enacted during the Great Depression was the National Labor Relations Act (NLRA). Section 7 of the NLRA gives workers the right to form labor unions without employer interference and compels employers to bargain collectively with unions chosen by the employees. A federal agency, the National Labor Relations Board (NLRB), was established by the NLRA to investigate employer violations of the act and to conduct elections in which workers can freely choose whether or not they want to be represented by a union.

Since the passage of the NLRA, the vast majority of unions have been formed through NLRB-conducted *representation elections.* This is not to say that a union cannot be formed through direct actions. But the law itself places serious roadblocks in the path of direct actions, so chances are that if you are ever part of a unionization effort, you will use the NLRB or some similar agency.[15] The NLRA does not cover all employees. Farm workers, domestic workers, railroad and airline workers, and public employees are the most important groups not covered. However, Congress and many state legislatures have passed laws similar to the NLRA which protect these workers. For example, railroad and airline workers can use the Railway Labor Act to get a union, and state and local government workers in most states can use state public employee laws. Therefore, the procedure described below for those covered by the NLRA will also be useful for most of the uncovered workers.

The principles underlying the NLRA are that, first, if a *majority* of workers in a workplace want a union, they should have a way to get one without having to engage in direct actions, and, second, only one union should represent any particular group of workers. Further, the workers who decide to form a union must have common interests, by, for example, doing the same type of work. These workers form the *bargaining unit.*

Once the workers have carved out a bargaining unit, they must convince the NLRB that there is a sufficient interest in unionization to warrant an NLRB election. The board uses the yardstick that 30 percent of the members of the shop must express an interest in being represented by a particular union. This means that the workers must affiliate themselves with a union. They could constitute themselves as an independent union; glass factory workers could form the "Meadville Glassworkers Union," or some similar organization. However, it will probably be wiser for employees to contact an already existing union to help them organize. This is because winning an election or forcing the employer to recognize the union without an election is a time-consuming, expensive undertaking. Unions have organizers, legal staffs, and money, all of which may be essential for victory.

Great care must be taken in choosing a union. Although many unions today know that they must organize new members or die, it is still the case that too many unions devote too little effort to organizing. So when workers make contact with a union, they should ask questions and get assurances that the union will do right by them. For example, the workers at the Borders bookstore in the World Trade Center in Manhattan, who recently voted in favor of a union, asked the local Jobs with Justice, a grassroots labor rights organization, to recommend a good union for them. Jobs with Justice suggested the United Food and Commercial Workers Local 888, an ethnically, racially, and sexually diverse union which had been aggressively organizing a wide variety of workers in the area. The glass workers in Meadville chose the Aluminum, Brick, and Glass Workers (ABG), which has won contracts from major glass manufacturers. The ABG has since merged with the United Steelworkers of America (USWA), a very large union which has committed itself to organizing and has a large and sophisticated staff. But while size and staff are important, experience in the industry is critical as well. For example, the United Auto Workers (UAW) failed to organize the glass workers at the sister plant in Carlisle, Pennsylvania, despite the fact that it had the early support of 80 percent of the bargaining unit.

The typical way in which workers show interest in unionization is by signing *union authorization cards;* these state that each worker authorizes the union to represent them for purposes of collective bargaining. The union can petition the NLRB for an election once 30 percent of the members of the bargaining unit have signed the cards, although no union should ever go into an election without at least 50 percent of the cards signed—and probably a lot more. Not everyone who signs a card will wind up voting for the union. Another way to show the necessary support for the union is for the workers to sign a petition, which can also be presented to the NLRB instead of, or along with, authorization cards. As a tactic, this is actually better than signing cards, because each person signing a petition will see the other names on it, whereas card signing is a private matter. To win an election, workers have to publicly commit themselves to the union, and a petition forces them to do this.

Once the requisite number of cards have been signed, the union petitions the NLRB for an election. The board notifies the employer. At this point, the employer is free to recognize the union or consent to an election. Most employers will do neither of these things. Instead they will ask the board to conduct a hearing, at which the union must show that it has enough support for an election and in which it will have to show appropriate basis for the bargaining unit. Employers often use these hearings just to delay the union drive and give them more time to develop their anti-union efforts. In addition, the employer may be able to convince the board that the bargaining unit is not appropriate; it may have jobs in it which are beyond its proper scope, or it may not include enough workers. The university at which I work once held up union elections for more than two years by continually challenging the bargaining unit.

If the union successfully makes its case, the board will set a date (or dates) for the election. The employer is then free to try vigorously to get the workers to vote against the union. Amendments to the original NLRA, as well as NLRB and court decisions, have greatly expanded the range of anti-union activities which an employer can use. Often employers hire consultants to run their anti-union campaigns, and many of these are notorious for their semi-legal and illegal tactics.[16] But even the legal tactics are appalling. Under current law it is legal for an employer to:

• Barrage the workers with anti-union propaganda, including letters (even videos) to the employees and their families at their homes. This propaganda does not have to be true, and as long as it is not directly threatening, it can suggest that certain bad things will happen if the workers vote in the union.

• Assign supervisors to engage in daily face to face "discussions" with union supporters.

• Prohibit union organizers who are not employees from being anywhere on company property.

• Hold *captive audience* meetings at the workplace. At these mandatory meetings, supervisors will pull out all of the stops to convince the workers that disaster awaits them if they vote for a union. They will tell the workers to give them another chance and things will get better. An organizer told me that one boss actually pulled out a handkerchief with an onion hidden in it, so that he could look like he was crying during one of these spiels.

Most employers will go further and commit illegal acts during the union campaign; they will transfer workers who support the union, threaten them, offer them bribes, or even fire them in order to defeat the union. Under current law, the penalties for such dirty tricks usually come too late and hurt the employer too little to make a difference. One researcher has found that since the passage of the North American Free Trade Agreement (NAFTA), employers have more frequently threatened to move their plants to Mexico or close them if a union won an election.[17]

On the election date, the workers vote by secret ballot. The union must win 50 percent plus one of the votes cast to be certified by the NLRB as the *sole bargaining agent* for the workers. If the union loses, it can challenge the results if the employer has violated the law by committing *unfair labor practices*. The board will hold a hearing and has the power to overturn the election results. If it does, it may simply order another election. It can also overturn the election and order the employer to recognize the union despite the lost election, but that does not happen very often—only when the employer has so egregiously violated the law that the board feels that a fair election can no longer be held. Once the union has been certified as the bargaining agent, it has the duty to notify the employer that it wants to negotiate a contract with the employer.

SUCCESSFUL UNION ORGANIZING

It is difficult to force an employer to recognize a union, despite the protections supposedly provided by the labor laws. Over the past thirty years, unfair labor practices by employers have mushroomed, and union victory rates in elections have declined. For example, the unfair labor practices most germane to union election campaigns rose fourfold between the early 1950s and 1990, while refusals to bargain increased eightfold during the same period. In the 1950-1954 period, unions won 72.1 percent of NLRB elections, but by 1990 this ratio had fallen to 49.5 percent. Today it is closer to 45 percent, and the number of employees in newly certified bargaining units has steadily decreased, from more than half a million in the early period to fewer than eighty thousand now.[18] Empirical studies indicate that employers' tactics, including the illegal ones, have a negative impact on union success rates.[19]

Yet it is not impossible for unions to win recognition from employers. Some unions have decided to organize unions outside of the National Labor Relations Act. They do this in a variety of ways, usually involving direct actions. The United Food and Commercial Workers tries to organize boycotts against stubborn employers, telling them, in effect, that the boycotts will be ended when the employer recognizes the union.[20] Others focus attention upon an entire community, trying to raise citizen awareness of the rights of workers and participating actively in community life. Then, when particular employers are targeted for organization, the union has already built a favorable climate which the employer will have difficulty combatting. A union might then hold an ad hoc representation election under the supervision of a community organization, and if the workers vote for the union, community pressures can be brought to bear upon the employer to recognize it.[21]

No matter whether unions organize under the NLRA or not, we have a good deal of evidence about what it takes for a union to succeed.[22] To overcome the obstacles employers and the law put in the path of union organizing, union tactics matter. In fact, researchers Kate Bronfenbrenner and Tom Juravich say

Workers locked out of A. E. Staley plant sprayed with pain-inducing peppergas by police, Decatur, Illinois, 1994. (Jim West)

that "union tactics as a group played a greater role in explaining election outcome than any other group of variables, including employer characteristics and tactics, bargaining unit demographics, organizer background, or election environment."[23]

A successful union often takes time to build. Those workers who strongly support the union must, with the help of the union's organizers, build a rank-and-file organization inside the workplace right from the beginning. This means meeting and talking with coworkers to build understanding and support long before asking them to sign petitions or authorization cards.

We often think of unions as organizations whose only purpose is to get their members more money. Yet Bronfenbrenner and Juravich found, "Unions which focus on issues such as dignity, justice, discrimination, fairness, or service quality were associated with higher win rates than those which focused on more traditional bread and butter issues, such as wages, benefits, and job security."[24] The sanitation workers on strike in Memphis, Tennessee, whom Martin Luther King, Jr. was supporting at the time of his assassination in 1968, wore signs which said "I Am a Man." The women clerical workers who organized Yale organized Yale University in the 1970s wanted respect and dignity, plus an end to racial and sexual discrimination, and not merely more pay.[25]

To acheive these goals, a "culture of solidarity" must permeate every aspect of the union drive. In general terms, the employer must come to be understood as the "class enemy" of the workers, one that can be defeated only if the workers stick together, acting as if "an injury to one is an injury to all." The union should encourage a gradual escalation of solidarity actions through which the workers will discover through action that unity is both possible and beneficial. For example, once an internal organizing committee is formed, its members can begin to have informal meetings with other workers outside of the plant or arrange to visit workers at their homes. Then a petition of union support might be circulated. Signing a petition might be the first step in getting a person's commitment; once it is obtained the worker's further commitment should be invited and secured. Once sufficient numbers have signed a petition, a rally of signers might be organized; an open rally means people stand up for what they have done and makes further actions easier. Regular events, from meetings with speakers to social events, can further solidify the workers. People must be made aware at these events of what the employer is doing or will be doing to undermine the union effort. It is relatively easy for the union to predict the employer's tactics, since they all use basically the same ones. In addition, the workers' families and the larger working community must be brought into the campaign from the beginning. Workers from other union bargaining units can be excellent organizers, since they speak from direct experience. As soon as possible, workers should begin to formulate the demands which they will bring to the bargaining table when their union drive succeeds. Perhaps demands can be presented to the employer before the election.

In their research, Bronfenbrenner and Juravich found that the following specific tactics were especially helpful in winning elections:

1. Forming an organizing committee. This workplace committee should include as high a percentage of workers as possible. It should be representative of the composition of the workforce in as many ways as possible. Each department of the workplace should be represented, and the sexual and racial composition of the committee should reflect those of the workplace as a whole.

Optimally, the union staff people will also reflect these compositions. For example, in plants with mostly Asian women workers, the organizers should be Asian women, or at least women familiar with their circumstances. Similarly, organizing in the South requires unions to use African-American organizers, since it is still the case that most African-American workers labor in the South. Those who originally form the organizing committee should make a diagram of the workplace to aid in the organizing.

2. **House calling.** Successful unionization demands face-to-face contacts. For example, I have participated in four failed attempts to unionize the teachers at the college at which I work. One of the reasons why these efforts failed is because the teachers would not speak directly to their co-workers even at work. College teachers are too caught up in the middle-class view that it is not polite to infringe upon another person's privacy. It was unthinkable for many union supporters to buttonhole their colleagues in the hallways, much less in their homes. Therefore the union relied too heavily upon mass mailings and letters to newspapers. We had missed the point that the formation of a union is an emotional as well as an intellectual experience. Getting people to take actions which they have been taught all of their lives are not appropriate requires that they be moved, that they get angry, that they come to see that there are principles at stake. Only through personal contact is there any hope of winning the emotional commitment without which a union cannot succeed. House calling should be done by union-supporting workers as well as organizers, for the obvious reason that potential recruits are bound to be more receptive to people whom they recognize.

3. **Holding mass and small group meetings.** Unions are collective organizations and as such require regular meetings to work effectively and democratically. At meetings, not only can workers hear what the union is all about, they can also learn the fundamentals of democratic organization and begin to gain the confidence which will help them confront their employers. Meetings can also be social events, places at which workers can solidify friendships and make new ones. At larger meetings, people from other workplaces can inform the workers of how unions have benefitted them and can help the new union develop its strategies.

4. Using solidarity days, on which union supporters do something to show their solidarity. At the Meadville glass factory, the workers showed their unity, pride, and dignity by wearing red union t-shirts. Depending on circumstances, a solidarity day can also be an occasion to challenge managerial authority in a more direct way, such as a group of union supporters formally grieving some particularly outrageous management action.

5. Forming a bargaining committee before the election. People begin to see that something may become a possibility as they actually begin to do it. As workers develop concrete contract proposals, their ingenuity is tapped and they become impatient that their proposals are not already the law of the shop. The idea is to make unionization a more or less self-fulfilling prophesy.

Not only do such tactics make it possible to win unionization even when the employer vigorously resists the workers' efforts, but they are crucial to the union winning a first contract. Management does not stop fighting the union once it wins the election. It will try to prevent the union from getting the critical first collective bargaining agreement, and it will succeed about a third of the time. It will do so by using legal and illegal tricks to delay the bargaining; to detect and to prevent this, the union must continue to build the rank-and-file movement after the election. Finally, to be effective, a union must convince most or all of the members of the bargaining unit to actually become members of the union. Under current labor laws, it is not possible to negotiate a contract provision which forces workers to become union members.[26] However, the tactics which work in organizing and in bargaining also work in building union membership.

CHAPTER THREE

UNION STRUCTURES AND DEMOCRACY

In the 1996 presidential election, Republican candidate Bob Dole, no friend of working people, repeatedly disparaged the union "bosses" who were supporting President Clinton. What made this remarkable is that Dole, like Clinton, got most of his money from corporate officials—who really are bosses! Yet he would never have thought to call them "bosses." Unions are routinely accused of being undemocratic bureaucracies, more interested in enriching their leaders than in serving their members. Union leaders are often referred to as "bosses," even by those who are generally sympathetic to unions. Working people often tell pollsters that they believe that union leaders are not trustworthy.[1]

Is it true that unions are top-down organizations with bosses, just like the corporations that they claim to be fighting? While it is true that many unions are not as democratic as they should be, there is no doubt that unions, especially at the local level, are among the most democratic institutions in the country. And even the most top-down union has a *potential* for democracy that every employer lacks. General Motors is organized as a hierarchy with orders emanating from the top and carried out below, and this is true of most employers, both private and public. If the board of directors of GM decides that the corporation is going to do a certain thing, there is no way that the employees can bring about a change in the corporation's hierarchy to reverse the change. The workers do not elect the board members, nor do they have the power to force a change so that they could elect them. In other words, most employers do not have democratic organizations, and they cannot be made to have them.

The power is at the top, supported by the property rights of the owners and the government which stands ready to enforce them.

In a union, the situation is much different. Unions are organizations which workers have formed voluntarily and in such a way that they, the members, have or can exert real power. All unions have constitutions or bylaws which provide for democratic structures, and important federal laws promote union democracy. This is not to say that all unions act democratically, but they all have a democratic potential utterly absent in employers. History gives us all too many examples of undemocratic, even corrupt, unions, although it also gives us plenty of examples of union democracy. However, there are no unions in which democracy is completely absent. Consider the International Brotherhood of Teamsters, the union that comes to everyone's mind when the words "corrupt union" are spoken. For at least fifty years this union was mired in corruption, controlled by organized criminals who used its pension funds as banks for their casinos in Las Vegas. Yet the national Teamsters union was comprised of hundreds of local unions which were not corrupt and which carried out the wishes of their members. In Minneapolis in the late 1930s the Teamsters led one of the great labor rebellions of the Great Depression, establishing a model of democratic and progressive unionism in the process.[2] And in the early 1980s and 1990s courageous reformers built a rank-and-file movement called Teamsters for a Democratic Union (TDU), whose aim was to win back control of the union for the members. They stood up to the gangsters and their union stooges and eventually succeeded in getting the federal government to press racketeering charges against them. The government also agreed to oversee open and fair elections. As a result reformer Ron Carey and his allies in the TDU won control of the union and began to implement an ambitious program of democratic reforms.

Of course, there are many problems yet to be solved; only this year Carey won reelection against the son of the legendary (and corrupt) Jimmy Hoffa by a slim margin. Then, in a tragic turn of events, Carey himself was accused of using union funds to aid his election, in a scheme that funneled money from the union to certain liberal organizations which then gave the money to Carey's campaign. It appears that the Democratic Party and AFL-CIO officials were also involved. Carey was forced by the government overseer to step down as

Diana Kilmury (front left) leads TDU members in demanding democracy at the Teamsters convention, Las Vegas, 1981. (Jim West)

president and disqualified from running again. Given that chicanery is commonplace in political campaign financing, the penalty against Carey may seem excessive. But a union must be controlled by its rank-and-file and not by its bureaucrats. And a labor movement must be politically independent and not in league with its class enemies in any political party.

Yet despite this terrible turn of events, the Teamsters union has been radically changed by the efforts of the TDU, in a way which would be utterly impossible in a privately owned business or government agency.[3] You can bet that the recently won UPS strike, carried out under Carey's leadership, would never have occurred under the Teamsters' old guard, which probably would have signed a sellout contract with the company. It will be up to the TDU and its rank-and-file allies to continue to fight for democracy in the union, irrespective of who the officers happen to be.

LOCALS AND INTERNATIONALS

When workers form a union they usually form a *local* of a larger national or international. (Some U.S. unions are called *internationals* because they have members and locals in Canada.) The union will have a constitution to which the local must subscribe, but the local will also have its own bylaws which will be binding for all local members. The bylaws will establish which officers the union will have and how they are to be selected, and the local's rules of operations: who is eligible to run for office, whether or not the officers will be paid, the duties of the officers, the lengths of the terms of the officers, the frequency and times of the union's meetings, the behaviors expected of union members, the dues of the local (these may be specified in part by the national or international union), etc. In the United States there are thousands of local unions, almost all of which are members of national or international unions.[4] There are a few independent locals unattached to a national or international. In some cases, these independents are closely allied with the employer and may be *company unions;* they do not independently pursue the interests of the workers.

While there is a lot of diversity in union structures, in the most common structure, the local union has a good deal of autonomy but is bound to the rules and policies of the national or international union of which it is a member. A union may also contain intermediate bodies between the levels of the local and the national. For example, the American Federation of Teachers (AFT), of which I was a member for many years, is a national union of school teachers and related workers. My local was called the United Faculty (most locals are simply designated by their numbers, as in Local 3 of the International Brotherhood of Electrical Workers). We had our own constitution and bylaws and, in general, set our own policies. We had not yet won bargaining rights, but if we had, we would have established our own bargaining agenda. As part of the AFT, we were required to pay a part of our dues (called the *per capita*) to an intermediate group, the Pennsylvania Federation of Teachers, and to the national union itself. The role of the state federation is to service the locals, publish a newspaper, form alliances with other unions in the state, and act as a lobbying group with the state legislature. This last role is of great importance for teachers, most of whom are public employees and whose employers are, therefore, dependent upon the state for funding. The national union sets the overall program of the union, hires a staff of researchers, organizers, lawyers, lobbyists, and the like, who service the locals, help the union to secure new members, lobby various political bodies, and promote public support for teachers and education.

The most common schema, therefore, is: local—intermediate body—national. However, even within this structure there is a lot of variability.[5] First, local union autonomy varies from union to union. Some locals might be able to call strikes irrespective of the wishes of the national officers, while others might have to first secure the approval of the national union. Some unions have large strike funds, and before a local's members can gain access to it, they must get permission to strike from the national. Second, locals vary enormously in size and in the complexity of their tasks. A local union of electrical workers may represent all of the electrical workers in a large city and may negotiate with an association of construction contractors. These contractors may contribute money into a pension fund—so many cents for each hour a union electrician is employed by one of them—and the local union may help to manage a large pension fund. By contrast, a local union of GM automobile workers would not be involved in pension fund management; the national would attend to that.

Third, unions differ in how they select their officers. Local officers are normally selected by secret ballot by the members. The officers, then, may have the power to appoint staff. In a factory setting, the first-level union official, the one in most direct contact with the members at the workplace, is called the *shop steward*. In some unions, stewards are elected, while in others they are appointed by the officers. The same thing might be true of the local's bargaining committee.

Intermediate body and national officers are usually chosen in one of two ways. They are either elected by the direct vote of the membership or they are elected by delegates to the national union's periodic conventions. The delegates are local union officers, appointed staff persons, or some combination of the two. Both systems can be democratic, although the direct election method is the most democratic and therefore the most desirable. Before the reform of the Teamsters union, for example, national officers were elected by delegates to the national convention, but most of the delegates were appointed staff persons. Such a situation, in which it is nearly impossible to unseat an incumbent union officer, is tailor-made for corruption.

Most of the more than one hundred national and international unions in the United States are, in turn, a part of a still larger federation of unions, the American Federation of Labor and Congress of Industrial Organizations (AFL-CIO). In some ways the relationship between the AFL-CIO and its member unions is similar to the relationship between a national union and its locals. The AFL-CIO publishes a newspaper; it has a large staff of researchers; it hires organizers and sponsors an "Organizing Institute"; it has a contingent of lobbyists in Washington, D.C.; and in general it acts as the spokesperson for working people. However, the AFL-CIO has limited powers over the affiliated national unions; these maintain their autonomy. The AFL-CIO can try to work out disagreements among the member unions, getting them to agree not to raid each others' members, for example. But it cannot dictate policies to them. If a national union wants to end a strike, the AFL-CIO cannot prevent it from doing so, even if its officers believe that the union is making a bad mistake. The AFL-CIO can, of course, expel unions from membership, and it has done this a few times, most notably at one point when it expelled the Teamsters for corruption, a decision since rescinded. And not all national unions are members of the federation. The nation's largest teachers' union, the National Education Association, is not a member (although a merger of the NEA with the American Federation of Teachers, an AFL-CIO affiliate, is imminent), nor is the smaller United Electrical, Radio, and Machine Workers of America (UE). All in all, the AFL-CIO can best be described as a weak federation, which is good in terms of member union independence, but bad for forging united worker actions. It is of considerable importance, though, and we will have more to say about it later in the book.[8]

Within certain geographical areas, for example in cities, the AFL-CIO-affiliated unions form another kind of organization: *central labor councils.* These councils serve a variety of functions. Historically they have served as coordinators of local union organizing. Suppose that the United Steel Workers union is trying to organize a steel fabricating company in Pittsburgh, Pennsylvania. The unions in Pittsburgh's Central Labor Council could agree to support the organizing effort with money and organizers from the member unions. The council could support a boycott of the target company's products. In a strike, council unions could help with the picketing. Members of the unions could refuse to cross the picket lines to make deliveries or to do construction work on the struck premises. Central labor councils can sponsor labor education classes for union members or, indeed, for any workers in the area. In these ways central labor councils can help to build strong local labor movements. Unfortunately, while a few central labor councils still do these things, many of them are inactive and devote most of their energies to helping local charities such as the United Way, and to getting out the vote for labor-friendly candidates.[9]

UNION STRUCTURE AND THE LAW

While union structures exhibit much diversity, they all must conform to an important federal labor law, the Labor Management Reporting and Disclosure Act, more commonly known as the Landrum-Griffin Act.[6] This statute was enacted by Congress in 1959 in the wake of several Congressional investigations into union corruption. Since employers do not typically mind dealing with corrupt unions (which, incidentally, often make large contributions to the campaigns of conservative politicians), it follows that "corruption in unions" was a smokescreen for the real purpose of the hearings— to give all of labor a black eye. Employers and their governmental allies wanted to create the impression that unions were in fundamental conflict with their members, who needed protection from corrupt and autocratic union leaders. Yet, as is sometimes the case, the anti-union intentions of the Congressional investigators produced legislation of potentially great importance to union members.

The act is divided into a number of parts, or "titles," the most important provisions of which are the following:

• **Title I:** The union member's "bill of rights." It guarantees that a union cannot deny the rights provided by its constitution and bylaws to any member. No member can be denied the right to speak out at union meetings, to run for union office, or to have access to the union's newspaper. A union's president cannot arbitrarily replace a staff person who has been elected by the membership. A union cannot deny a member running for union office the right to place advertisements in the union paper if the incumbent has such a right. A member whose rights have been violated can sue the union in state court. Of great importance, "No member of any labor organization may be fined, suspended, expelled, or otherwise disciplined except for nonpayment of dues by such organization or by any officer thereof unless such member has been (a) served with written charges; (b) given a reasonable time to prepare his defense; (c) afforded a full and fair hearing."

• **Title II:** Unions must file various membership and financial reports with the Department of Labor, and all of this information must be made available to the members upon request.

• **Title III:** Strict limits are placed on the right of the national union to implement trusteeships. The constitutions of most national unions give them the power to temporarily take over the affairs of their locals or intermediate bodies. This is called putting the local in *trusteeship,* and it is not a bad thing if the local has fallen prey to gangsters or if local officers have stolen funds. However, in some unions, trusteeships were forced upon locals in order to consolidate the power of the national union's officers and to deny the democratic functioning of the locals. Title III stipulates against such abuses of power.

• **Title IV:** Unions must have regular elections of officers. Local unions must have such elections at least once every three years and national unions once every five years. All elections must conform to minimal democratic standards; for example, they must be by secret ballot. A union cannot establish discriminatory eligibility rules, such that, for example, a member had to be present at 90 percent of the union's meetings in the past year to be eligible for office. The Department of Labor, which administers most of the act, has the power to overturn a union election and to oversee a new one. This is what happened in the United Mine Workers in 1972. Incumbent Tony Boyle had won reelection in a tainted election in 1969. In fact, he had his main rival, Joseph "Jock" Yablonski, murdered right after that election. The Department of Labor, upon petition from Boyle's challengers, overturned the election, which paved the way for the election of Arnold Miller, the candidate of the miners' reform group, Miners for Democracy, and for the revival of democracy in that great union.[7]

AN EXAMPLE OF UNION DEMOCRACY

The United Electrical, Radio, and Machine Workers of America, better known as the UE, was one of the unions which built the movement of industrial unionism during the labor wars of the Great Depression.[10] A charter member of the pre-merger CIO, the UE had, by the end of the Second World War, organized most of the large firms which produced both industrial and consumer electronic goods, most notably General Electric and Westinghouse. The UE established an admirable record of both rank-and-file democracy and progressive politics, and, in the process, won significant gains in wages, hours, and working conditions for hundreds of thousands of electrical, machine, and radio workers. Unfortunately the union fell victim to the anticommunist frenzy of the Cold War. The UE was ultimately expelled from the CIO because its officers would not sign the non-communist oaths required by the Taft-Hartley laws. Taft-Hartley, passed in 1947, amended the National Labor Relations Act, adding many anti-labor provisions to it. Taft-Hartley required that all union officers sign oaths stating that they were not members of the U.S. Communist Party, at the time a perfectly legal political party. Not only was this a violation of civil liberties, but it served to drive the left out of the unions. Communist Party members and supporters had done yeoman work in establishing the CIO, often taking the greatest risks and doing the most difficult organizing, and had gained considerable influence in some of the CIO unions, including the UE.[11] Especially noteworthy was the Communist position on the rights of African-American workers; radicals in the unions led the way in organizing black workers, most of whom worked in the South.[12] The left-led unions struggled and won collective bargaining agreements second to none in the industrial unions.

After the UE was purged from the CIO, other unions raided its members, a practice made easier by the denial to the UE of the protections of the NLRA and the NLRB and by the constant harassment of the employers and the red-hunters in Congress. Yet somehow the union survived, and after losing most of its members in the 1950s began a comeback in the next three decades. Today the union has about forty thousand members and is headquartered in Pittsburgh, a city which has seen some of the greatest UE victories and defeats. It no longer organizes only within the industries indicated in its name, but, like most unions today, will organize any workers who agree with its principles. Recently it organized janitors at the University of North Carolina in Chapel Hill, and the UE is planning a campaign to organize all such workers in all of the public colleges and universities in the state. The vitality of the union is partly explained by its vibrant internal democracy—which some other unions should implement in order to strengthen themselves.

The UE has a tripartite organizational structure.[13] At the top there is the national union. The constitution of the national union states that the object of the union is "to protect, maintain, and advance the interests of working people, to organize local unions at places of employment, and to promote the advancement of such bodies." The union seeks to organize any private and public sector workers "who desire organization on the basis of rank and file control in order to pursue a policy of aggressive struggle to improve their conditions." The union promises to accept members irrespective of their "skill, age, sex, nationality, color, race, religious or political belief or affiliation, sexual orientation, or immigration status." The constitution provides for the election of a general president, general secretary-treasurer, director of organization, and a general vice-president for each of the union's geographical districts. These officers comprise the union's general executive board, which is responsible for the running of the national union. In addition, there are three trustees and two alternates who audit the union's books, take a yearly inventory, and generally safeguard all of the union's properties.

The national officers of the UE serve only one-year terms and must stand for election at the yearly convention of the union. The delegates to the convention are selected by the locals of the union by secret ballot of members in good standing. The delegates elected have voting power in proportion to the membership of their locals, but no local can have more than ten delegates irrespective of its number of members. Thus this union guarantees that the officers will be elected democratically, and it also protects the voice of smaller locals. This is in contrast to many other unions, which although they operate in a reasonably democratic manner, often allow convention delegates to be appointed by national officers, thereby making it difficult for alternative points of view to be heard. Even when the UE was being ripped apart by anticommunist dissidents, often sponsored by outside groups, it maintained its standard of spirited and democratic debates. Perhaps most remarkably, its constitution places strict limits on the salaries of the officers: "Where not defined in the Constitution, the General Executive Board may fix the compensation to be paid to any officer, member, or other person employed by the National Union provided that such compensation shall not exceed the maximum weekly wage paid in the industry. . . ." In 1996, the president of the union could be paid no more than $36,825.36. In this way the union makes sure that the officers stay close to the members and identify with them, as opposed to the employers with whom they negotiate. The constitution also provides another check on the officers. Any of them can be recalled through a petition procedure initiated by the locals.

Beneath the national union (organizationally, that is, not in terms of power) are twelve district councils organized geographically. The goal of each council is to "secure mutual protection, harmonious action, and close cooperation among all locals within a given district, in all matters relating to the United Electrical, Radio and Machine Workers of America (UE)." The local unions elect the officers of the councils. Each council must have its own constitution. The one for district six, which covers the region in which I live, is pretty much patterned after the national union constitution, with an emphasis on rank-and-file control and maximum democracy.

The base of the union consists of the local unions in each district. Each local must have a constitution, which spells out the number of officers, the duties of the officers, the times of the local's meetings, the local's standing committees, the dues structure, the procedures for calling strikes, and the rights of a member brought up on charges by another member for violating the union's rules and regulations. Each of the constitutions (national, regional, and local) includes procedures to guarantee basic due process rights to any accused member. The national constitution provides for the chartering of new locals, and the basic dues structure is established by the national convention. Today a local can charge between ten and twenty dollars per week for dues, and five dollars of this goes to the national office.

In the UE, strikes are called by the locals, although any strike must be in conformity to the union's constitution. Specifically, "Any strike related to the negotiation of a new collective bargaining contract or the renewal of an existing collective bargaining contract and all contract settlements must be approved by vote of the membership of the local or locals involved. . . ." Each local must establish a strike defense fund to support members when they are on strike. In collective bargaining, "No representative of the United Electrical, Radio and Machine Workers of America (UE) shall negotiate alone with the employer."

The UE goes to great lengths to insure that the members actually control the union, from the national convention to the daily operations of every level of the union. Article 25 of the national constitution is titled "UE Rank-and File Principles," which includes the following statement: "The UE staff is employed by the membership through the national officers and general executive board and implements the leadership's decisions to build the union membership, to assist the locals and districts in solving their problems, and to effectuate UE programs and policies. Staff members have no right to interfere with UE rank-and-file control, including election processes, at any level of the union. To deviate from this policy would lead to a staff-controlled union."

Naturally a union may not act as democratically as its constitution might suggest, but the UE has, in fact, operated throughout its history in accord with its principles, and therefore it can serve as a measuring rod for the evaluation of other unions. A few unions do provide for greater due process for union members charged with a violation of union rules. The United Auto Workers (UAW) has an independent review board to which a member can appeal an adverse ruling. But the UAW is much more dominated by its staff than is the UE. In many unions today there are rank-and-file movements which are insisting on greater union democracy, and the labor movement will succeed in rebuilding itself only to the extent that these movements achieve success.

A LOCAL UNION MEETING

For many years, I was a member of the American Federation of Teachers (AFT). My local was named the United Faculty, and our goal was to organize the teachers at the University of Pittsburgh, which is where I work. Every aspect of our union was democratic. We wrote our own constitution and bylaws, and we made our own decisions with respect to our strategies and policies. The AFT has state federations and a national office, and we were affiliated with both the Pennsylvania Federation of Teachers and the AFT. We set our own dues, but we had to pay a "per capita" amount of money to both the

(Carol/Simpson)

state and national federations as well as to the AFL-CIO, with which the AFT was affiliated. The AFT provided us with funds for our organizing drives as well as with organizers and staff. Of course, we were bound by the AFT's constitution and the AFT could decide not to back our efforts, but all in all, the local ran with a remarkable amount of autonomy. Eventually the AFT agreed to a merger of our AFT local with that of another union, the American Association of University Professors (AAUP), and so we were a sort of joint union.

We held our meetings in a building owned by a Protestant church, which was used for a variety of purposes. These meetings were run according to a standard form, with any member present free to speak his or her mind about any issue brought forward. We made our decisions by vote of our executive board or by a mail ballot of the entire membership, depending on the issue and the rules in our constitution. There were times when the meetings were very routine, and there were times when the meetings got quite heated. We had many disagreements with the AFT staff and sometimes with our attorneys. We did not always like the positions taken by the national AFT. But our union was always an exercise in democracy, and much the same can be said of the operations of the vast majority of local unions.

If we look at the history of the labor movement, we discover that its periods of growth were the times when the movement came to symbolize a path to a better life for all working people. Researchers are now also finding that the more democratic the union movement, and the more militant and class conscious its leaders, the better off the workers end up being.[14]

CHAPTER FOUR

COLLECTIVE BARGAINING

Once a union has been formed, it seeks to establish the terms under which its members will work. Although unions used to simply set these conditions and refuse to work unless they were agreed to by the employer, today wages, hours, and terms and conditions of employment are normally worked out through a process known as *collective bargaining*. A union formally recognized by the employer, either because of an election or voluntarily by the employer, has the right to negotiate with the employer, and the employer has an obligation to do so. The National Labor Relations Act requires the employer to bargain in "good faith."[1] This does not mean that the employer must come to an agreement with the union, only that it have "intent" to reach agreement. The union is the sole bargaining agent for all of the people in the bargaining unit (whether they are members of the union or not); this means that the employer must bargain with this union, with no other, and not with individual workers.[2]

The process of reaching agreement with an employer, of arriving at a written collective bargaining agreement or contract, is difficult. Employers often engage in a variety of stalling tactics known as *surface bargaining*, that is, going through the motions of negotiating without having any real intent to reach agreement. They may cancel or delay meetings; they may agree to minor and costless union proposals but refuse to consider important ones; they may refuse to offer counterproposals to the union's demands; they may add new proposals just when it appears that agreement is close; and they may

Let's make a deal: UAW and GM representatives open 1984 negotiations.
(Jim West)

take back agreement on bargaining items already concluded. These tactics are illegal, in bad faith, but the labor laws do not have enough teeth to deter employers from using them. If the union files an unfair labor practice grievance, it may be many months before the NLRB or a related agency makes a ruling. In the meantime, the workers may become demoralized at the failure of the union to get a contract, and the employer will take advantage of this by blaming the delay on the unreasonableness of the union. In addition, there is turnover in any workplace, so some union supporters may quit, retire, get injured, or die, all of which will sap the union's strength. Worst of all, if the board does rule against the employer, the typical penalty is simply for the employer to be ordered back to the bargaining table. There is no monetary penalty for an employer's refusal to bargain in good faith.

The weakness of the law has led to a sharp rise in refusals to bargain and other unfair labor practices. Between the early 1950s and the beginning of the 1990s, these increased by nearly eight times, which is all the more discouraging since union membership was declining throughout most of this period.[3] The most important consequence of employer lawlessness is that it has become much more difficult for a new union to win its first collective bargaining agreement. In fact, nearly one-third of all first negotiations end without the union achieving an agreement with the employer. In other words, although the union wins recognition, it is ultimately defeated.[4] The situation is not so bad for established unions, although even here a refusal to bargain can have serious consequences, especially if the union is not prepared or able to force the employer back to the bargaining table.

This means that if a union is to win a good agreement, it must approach bargaining in the same way it approached the initial organizing. All of the tactics which researchers have found essential to successful organizing are also necessary for collective bargaining: one-on-one meetings, solidarity days, house-calling, rank-and-file-mobilization, and, above all, skillful preparations.

THE IWW'S CASE AGAINST COLLECTIVE BARGAINING

The American Federation of Labor, the trade union association created in the late nineteenth century, was mostly made up of unions of skilled or craft workers. These workers, overwhelmingly male and concentrated in particular ethnic groups (German, Irish, Jewish, etc.), often had disdain for unskilled workers, who were much more ethnically and racially diverse and contained a higher proportion of women. The AFL made little effort to organize the unskilled. In addition, while skilled workers were willing to utilize militant actions such as strikes and boycotts to force employers to deal with them, once they achieved a stable union they placed most of their efforts on negotiating contracts. The AFL's conservative approach to unionism, which included an acceptance of the wage system and a willingness to work within the two-party political framework, won it the enmity of more radical elements within the labor movement. Such radicals, led by men like Eugene Debs and Bill Haywood and women like Elizabeth Gurley Flynn, formed other kinds of unions. The most famous of these was the Industrial Workers of the World, better known as the IWW or the Wobblies. Founded in 1905, the IWW had a base among hard rock miners in the West and agricultural, lumber, garment, and other highly exploited workers around the country.[5]

The IWW did not believe in craft unions or collective bargaining. Instead it favored "one big union" for all workers regardless of skill or any other factor, including race and sex. And it championed direct actions such as strikes, mass demonstrations, sit-ins, and sabotage of the employer's property. Bargaining and contracts could, in the Wobbly view, only serve to create a union bureaucracy whose job it would be to enforce the contract and prevent the members from using direct actions to protest the employer's actions. Instead it would be better if the workers enforced their will upon the employer by always standing ready to act together to force the employer into submission.

The IWW did organize some of the nation's most downtrodden workers, and it helped workers win some spectacular strikes. Wobbly agitators helped to make free speech a reality for working people by "soapboxing," unannounced public speeches in parks and on street corners in towns across the nation. Usually these would be broken up when the police made mass arrests. But ultimately the IWW was defeated by a combination of employer and government violence, AFL antagonism, and its own internal weaknesses. Its small remnant still exists, and Wobblies continue to play important roles in a variety of worker campaigns, including living wage struggles in places like Duluth, Minnesota.

Some unionists continue to believe that collective bargaining is a conservative strategy likely to discourage worker solidarity. A cogent argument has been made, for example, that the NLRA, with its strong discouragement of militant collective actions such as strikes and its encouragement of collective bargaining, helped to set the stage for the gradual takeover of the mass workers' movement of the early 1930s by labor bureaucrats. That is, the government agreed that workers could form unions, but in return it and the employers expected union leaders to police their members so that they would obey the contracts, filing grievances instead of taking direct actions to settle disputes.[6]

On the other hand, the IWW's contempt for collective bargaining made it more vulnerable to employer and government attacks by making every victory wholly dependent on its own members' reserves.

STRATEGIES OF THE CONTRACT CAMPAIGN

When unions were more powerful in the United States, collective bargaining was sometimes an elaborate ritual. In the 1950s, for example, the United Steelworkers of America (USWA) represented most of the workers who labored in the nation's steel mills. The union had won contracts from each of the large steel corporations, using the agreement settled with the largest producer, U.S. Steel, as the pattern contract for all of the other companies. These contracts were negotiated by a small group of national union officers and staff, without much input from the rank and file, who often did not know what was negotiated until they read the final agreement. The contracts were, in effect, imposed upon the members without any sort of ratification vote.[7] If the bargaining broke down, or reached what the labor law calls an *impasse,* the union would more than likely call a strike, and the workers would stay out until the company or the union conceded and an agreement was reached. The employers had little ability to hire replacement workers to break the strike, and sometimes all it took were token picket lines to enforce the strike.

Today the situation is much different. Decades of union decline, along with slack labor markets and a hostile legal environment, have given employers the advantage.[8] Today's companies are much more resistant to union demands and often come to the bargaining table with long lists of *give-backs* which they want from the workers. They do not necessarily mind strikes, seeing in them opportunities to hire replacement workers, draw down inventories, implement labor-saving technologies, and perhaps defeat the union once and for all. Unions like the United Auto Workers have been defeated by corporations like International Harvester, which just two decades ago would never have dared to challenge the union so strongly.[9] The old bargaining ritual is no longer viable, and unions have had to rethink how they go about bargaining. The best unions have come to see that negotiations must be approached as a *campaign,* with many battles and a wide array of tactics, all built upon the dedicated involvement of the members.

Say a union has been recognized by an employer and it wants to negotiate a contract. What happens next? First, the union must notify the employer of its desire to bargain; the employer is legally bound to do so. Then the union must commence its campaign. What follows is an outline of a strategy developed by the Service Employees International Union (SEIU) in its *Contract Campaign Manual.*[10]

Most people probably think of collective bargaining in terms of what goes on right around the bargaining table. The most skilled negotiators win, because, like good car salespersons, they know the tricks of the trade. But what really matters is *power*. While what goes on at the table is important and workers can learn to be good bargainers, what happens outside of the bargaining room is far more important. The union must use the power it has effectively and develop more power by building a strong bargaining campaign. The power of a union derives from the fact that its members perform work without which the employer cannot function. As SEIU puts it, "The most important source of power we have as a union is the unity and organization of our members." Note the words "unity" and "organization." These things can never be taken for granted. In the normal course of events, workers may be divided in many ways: age, skill, sex, race, experience. And workers may be in a union, but this does not mean that they will function as an organization. Unity and organization have to be *built*, carefully and constantly.

In a contract campaign, the leaders of the union, in close collaboration with the members, can begin to establish unity and organization by preparing a planning document which lays out what the union proposes to do, how it plans to do it, and a timetable for the plan's elements. The best time to begin is right after an old agreement has been signed (in the case of a contract renewal) or when the organizing of the union begins (in the case of a first contract). A contract campaign cannot get up to speed in a few days; time is required to put everything in place. Goals have to be established, both for the immediate bargaining and the long term. To set goals, the union must engage in various types of research. Questions such as the following must be answered: Who are the members of the union? How do they differ in terms of age, seniority, race, sex, marital status, job titles, and pay levels? What problems do the members face at work? How has the last contract worked? What parts of it have led to grievances or informal complaints? What changes in the workplace do the members want? What is the financial status of the employer? What types of relationships with suppliers, customers, banks, public officials, media, and so forth, are important to the employer? What does the union know about the managers of the plant and the company's negotiators?

Information can be gathered in various ways. The union can poll its members and conduct surveys, supported by one-on-one contacts, small group meetings, and union meetings. Most unions have research departments, and these can be used to get information, especially about the economic condition of the employer. The union will have a record of all grievances and arbitrations filed under the current agreement. Employers have to file a variety of reports, and these are often matters of public record; most of the records of public employers are also obtainable from the appropriate public agency. Reports may be available at the local courthouse (of lawsuits filed against the company or property transactions), the Internal Revenue Service (tax returns), or the Securities and Exchange Commission (various statements for stockholders). Government agencies such as the Bureau of Labor Statistics publish a wide range of reports on the overall economy and on specific industries, as well as wage and benefit trends. Private organizations such as the Bureau of National Affairs do similar research; the BNA publishes an annual "Source Book on Collective Bargaining" which contains much valuable information, including employer bargaining goals for the year and an update of legal changes.[11] Other unions, especially ones which have dealt with this employer, can supply information. They can also provide collective bargaining agreements for comparison. Newspapers, trade journals, magazines, and research papers should also be sought.

Employers themselves are an invaluable source of information. Some information can be gathered informally from friendly (often disgruntled) people inside management. Some data can be gotten through the company's annual report, which a union might get from a private company by purchasing a share of stock. However, the union has the legal right, simply by asking, to obtain from the employer any information which the union can reasonably claim is necessary for the union to fulfill its bargaining duties.[12] A union might make all sorts of demands at the bargaining table, from obvious ones like hourly wage rates, overtime, pensions, and vacations, to others like moving expenses, sexual harassment, successorship, and video display terminal policies. Upon request, the employer must provide the union with the data it has concerning these, and it is an unfair labor practice for the employer to refuse or fail to do so.

There are some exceptions. The labor law makes a distinction between *mandatory* and *permissive* bargaining subjects. Mandatory subjects are those about which the parties *must* negotiate; these include the ones just mentioned, as well as hundreds of others dealing with what the NLRB categorizes as "wages, hours, and terms and conditions of employment." Permissive bargaining subjects are those that the parties are not legally obliged to bargain, although they can if they so desire. A union does not have the right to request information concerning permissive subjects, nor can it try to force the employer to negotiate them by using pressure tactics such as strikes and boycotts. Generally speaking, a permissive subject is one which, as the courts have put it, goes to the heart of the managerial function. That is, the courts have ruled that management has certain inherent rights, simply because it represents those who own the property in the case of a private employer, or just because it is the management in the case of a public employer. Thus, a union cannot legally compel the employer to bargain about price of product, the selection of supervisors, the location of plants, the nature and types of product, a decision to close a plant, kinds of equipment used, the choice of health insurance carrier (as opposed to the level of health benefits), benefits for those already retired, and so forth.

Let us look at a couple of examples of when a union may want to request information. Suppose, as is often the case today, that the union suspects that the employer is going to seek to cut the costs of health insurance. The union can request at least the following: a copy of all health plans now in effect, employer and worker premium payments, administrative expenses, yearly cost to the employer per worker in total dollars and cents per hour, number of claims total and per employee, amounts of all claims, a distribution of the types of claims filed, complaints from employees about health insurance, any reports done by the employer or contracted by the employer concerning health care and costs, all utilization statistics, and complete patient data for each claim. Or suppose that the union wants to improve the employment circumstances of its female and minority members. It can request a list of all job classifications broken down by race and sex; any employer affirmative action plans, documents, and studies; reports filed to the EEOC or similar state agency; and copies of all materials relating to any discrimination lawsuits filed by employees. With so much information potentially available, it pays to do a little research on this aspect of the labor law.

Once the union has set its goals and fixed a timetable for achieving them, it must create an organizational structure which will be responsible for turning goals into reality. Committees must be formed, including a negotiating committee and a contract campaign committee; and various specialized committees as well, such as a media committee, a civil rights committee, and a childcare committee.

The negotiating committee will actually sit down and bargain with the employer. Legally, a union can have whomever it wants on this committee; the NLRA specifies "representatives of their [the workers'] own choosing." The union should make sure that this committee, like all others, is broadly representative of the bargaining unit, in terms of departments, age, sex, race, and any other categories which are important for this group of workers. If a workplace contains more than one union, it is often a good idea to have someone from one union be on the negotiating team of another. This can insure, among other things, that the employer does not try to play one group of workers off against another by spreading rumors about what is going on at the table. The members of this committee should be trained carefully; the use of role-playing is an especially useful technique for training negotiators.[13]

The job of the contract campaign committee is to mobilize the membership in a series of actions aimed at convincing the employer that the costs of not bargaining in good faith and ultimately reaching agreement are greater than doing the opposite. The committee is responsible for everything from organizing a phone tree for rapid communications to logistics for all campaign events. The key is to build up solidarity by beginning with relatively simple and easy actions and then moving to more aggressive and more risky tactics, all timed so as to maximize the value of each action. Again, the participation of the rank and file usually makes the difference between success and failure. Examples of pressure tactics inside of the workplace include wearing special union insignia; circulating petitions condemning some particularly urgent abuse; conducting "work-to-rule" slowdowns in which workers obey just the letter of their work rules and contract, and no more (bus drivers, for example, obeying all safety precautions exactly, thereby continuously running behind schedule); one-minute work stoppages; "rolling strikes" in which workers strike for a brief period, return to work, and strike again, or similar actions in which different departments strike at different times; and demonstrations in management offices.

Outside the workplace, the workers can begin a *corporate campaign,* in which they identify through their research the pressure points at which their employer is most vulnerable.[14] Perhaps the employers' customers can be reached through a consumer boycott. Perhaps the banks and insurance companies which provide financing to the employer can be pressured through techniques such as withdrawal of union funds and boycotts. In the case of a public employer, perhaps the politicians who make key decisions which affect the employer can be convinced to encourage the employer to settle. Nearly every employer is subject to a variety of regulations and laws, and not many of them can withstand close scrutiny of their compliance with these. Research might uncover, for example, that the employer is ignoring important safety and health regulations. These can be reported to the appropriate agency or court as well as to the media; the bad publicity received by the employer may pressure it to come to terms with the union. Most of these tactics can also be used in conjunction with other labor and community groups. Unions should maintain strong and reciprocal ties with all groups which might support them in their struggles with employers. Other unions might have relations with a certain employer, and their experience can be invaluable for a union dealing with that employer for the first time. Similarly a union will want the support of other unionized workers in cases of strikes, so that they do not cross picket lines. Community organizations, from churches to civil rights groups to environmental groups, can be convinced to make common cause with a union. Workers in a factory that is polluting a poor neighborhood are the natural allies of the local inhabitants whose health is being damaged.

Tactics must be coordinated in such a way that the employer experiences them as more and more threatening; the pressure must escalate. Suppose that this is a first agreement, and the employer argued throughout the campaign that the union was unlikely to win an agreement which improved the circumstances of the workers. As soon as—or even before—the election is won, or the employer otherwise recognizes the union, the union should initiate actions which demonstrate to the employer the seriousness of the workers. Workers could all wear special insignia to work, all of the time or on certain days; they could begin to present demands in small or large groups to supervisors; they could escalate to short work stoppages; they could build toward demonstrations timed to employer statements, or actions hostile to the bargaining; they could charge the employer with violations of laws and regulations, and distribute the facts to the media; they could hold a strike vote when the employer stalls in negotiations; they could picket on a regular basis during bargaining to alert the public to the situation.

One final point must be made about contract campaigns. The way in which these can be implemented, and whether implementation is easy or tough, will depend upon the *bargaining structure*.[15] When a single union local faces a one-plant employer, the structure is decentralized. If the workers in the bargaining unit all do the same type of work (for example, teachers), the structure is narrow, as opposed to a broad structure in which the unit consists of many different types of jobs (janitors, assemblyline workers, packers). In a highly centralized structure, the actual negotiators may be far removed from the workers. For example, when the Canadian Auto Workers union (CAW) negotiates with General Motors, it bargains on behalf of the workers at all of GM's plants in Canada. The union leader and a small inner circle of advisors do the bargaining with a top official of GM, and, in fact, a lot of the negotiations might be conducted one-on-one by these two officials. However, the inner circle must report back to a much larger group consisting of the presidents of all of the locals. Then the contract must be ratified by the workers themselves. The CAW is committed to securing good agreements for the members, and the overall structure of the union is democratic. In addition, the CAW strongly supports a progressive and independent labor politics.[16] So while the rank and file do not actually participate in the bargaining, they maintain a reasonably strong control of their union, and will remove from office any leaders not attuned to their needs. Unfortunately, not all centralized bargaining is done along the lines of the CAW, and history offers us numerous examples of union elites negotiating with their corporate counterparts in complete isolation from the members of the bargaining unit, often in situations in which the workers do not even have the right to ratify the final agreement. Hopefully, the new leadership of the AFL-CIO seems to be inclined toward a more democratic style of bargaining. In fact, the president of the AFL-CIO, John Sweeney, was formerly the president of SEIU, which developed a collective bargaining manual based upon contract campaigns. It is important to repeat, however, that in unions not controlled by the members, union leaders will not easily give up power to the rank and file. The members must organize themselves to insist that they do. The new leaders of organized labor may only be using the language of democracy to gain new members and leverage over employers without actually relinquishing any power. If this is the case, it will be up to union members to seize this opening toward democracy to construct real democracy in the labor movement.

BARGAINING IN WARTIME

The entry of the United States into the First World War in 1917 was not especially popular at first, and with good reason. The war was the consequence of intense economic and political rivalry for overseas markets and colonies. But the government made it extremely dangerous for workers to oppose it, making it clear that any opposition would be regarded as treasonous and actively prosecuting opponents under newly enacted wartime legislation. The AFL had earlier had a tradition of pacifism, but the federal government exerted strong pressure on it to support the war.[17] Eventually it agreed to support the war, and the government agreed to encourage employers to bargain collectively with AFL unions. As a consequence of this arrangement, the unions were committed not to strike during the war, union membership grew considerably, and unions won collective bargaining agreements.

There were those in the labor movement, notably the IWW and many socialists, who actively fought against the war. These people and organizations were persecuted and prosecuted by the government, which also turned a blind eye to the many private vigilante actions against war opponents mounted by groups such as the American Legion. Sadly, the AFL all too often cooperated with the authorities in these anti-radical attacks, which pretty much destroyed the left wing of the labor movement. Socialist leader Eugene V. Debs was sent to prison for ten years for making an anti-war speech in Ohio. IWW leader Big Bill Haywood was hounded out of the country and forced to seek refuge in the Soviet Union. So while the unions gained members and contracts during the war, the labor movement was dealt a serious blow, as those who took the most progressive stands on a wide range of social issues were literally expelled from the movement.[18]

Much the same thing happened during the Second World War. This war was much more popular than the First World War, and the purge of the radicals mostly took place after it. However, as in the previous war, the AFL and the CIO supported the war and its member unions pledged not to strike. And once again, the government placed strong pressure upon employers to recognize unions in their plants and to bargain collectively with them. The government sponsored a system of arbitration to settle contract disputes, as a substitute for strikes. This system of labor-management cooperation was put into place by top national union leaders, along with corporate and government bigwigs, with very little rank-and-file input. Union leaders got into the habit of sitting down with their corporate counterparts and working out settlements to their disputes without having to activate their members. Because of their allegiance to the Soviet Union, Communists in labor for the most part went along with this conservative arrangement. Radical politics and rank-and-file agitation were put on hold during the war, although workers did often strike in defiance of the no-strike pledge: the United Mine Workers, which did not concur with the pledge, actually conducted several nationwide work stoppages in 1943.[19]

After the war, the government and business went all out to crush the left wing of the labor movement.[20] This time the CIO unions did what the AFL had done during World War One and expelled the most radical and rank-and-file oriented unions, including the United Electrical Workers. This action marked the end of the mass movement of workers begun during the Great Depression. Bureaucratic, staff-dominated collective bargaining was extended after the war. A staff-controlled grievance procedure with arbitration as the final step used to resolve disputes became all but universal, and almost all collective bargaining agreements came to contain "no strike" agreements in which workers gave up the right to strike to settle workplace disagreements.

Some scholars have argued, as the IWW did, that modern collective bargaining is inherently bureaucratic and hostile to the interests of workers.[21] I take issue with this view. Both collective bargaining and grievance procedures can be of great advantage to workers. An effective collective bargaining campaign can permit unions time to regroup for battles to come. And a grievance procedure can be seen as just one more weapon to use in the ongoing war between employers and workers. Take the worker reinstated after being accused of falsifying a shoe reimbursement form. Ask him if he thinks that arbitration is inherently a bad thing for workers. Of course, arbitration today would be swifter and work more to the advantage of workers if labor had initially been bolder in its reactions to the great wars, but that should not discredit collective bargaining across the board.

AT THE TABLE

Hundreds of books have been written about the art and science of negotiations.[22] A reader of many of these tomes may be led to believe that anyone can negotiate anything, if only one learns the right "table skills." While it is important to do the right things at the bargaining table, collective bargaining occurs within a social context. A union which has prepared its membership to view the bargaining as part of an ongoing struggle will do better than one which fails to involve the members. With this in mind, there are some useful things for the negotiators to remember when they actually sit down to bargain.

The items that the union hopes to get into the final collective bargaining agreement are called *substantive* issues. Before negotiating these, the union must bargain *procedural* subjects. These are matters which spell out the procedures which the two parties are going to use to reach agreement. They include such things as the dates, places, and times of the meetings, whether the meetings will be tape-recorded, whether the negotiators agree not to take calls or leave the meeting room during the bargaining (except for caucuses), what relationships the bargainers will have with the media, whether or not attorneys will be present, how the parties will exchange information, how the sides will "agree that they have agreed," whether the meetings will take place during normal working hours, and, if so, whether the workers on the committee will be paid their regular wages. These are often crucially important points, and the union should give them the same care and preparation as the substantive issues. For example, the union should not agree to limit the people it can bring to the table, nor should it promise not to talk to the media. Most unions prefer to negotiate at a neutral site and not at the workplace, often a symbol of management's authority. The union should not agree to allow the employer to take care of the final preparation of the contract for printing, and it should be sure that it has good note-takers at each meeting.

At the table, the bargainers should maintain a tight discipline. It is not necessary that one person do all of the talking; it might be desirable to rotate the spokesperson each session to give as many people as possible this valuable experience. It is necessary, though, to anticipate and plan what will be said. The employer will be looking for signs of disagreement among the union's bargainers, so they should never show any such signs. Whenever there is disagreement or confusion among the union's negotiators, someone should call a caucus; that is, the union should say to the management that it wants to meet alone outside of the negotiating room. A good rule of bargaining is to always have a ready excuse to halt the bargaining. Away from the table, the team can get a clearer perspective of what is transpiring and not get caught up in a rush to reach agreement. Similar delaying tactics can be used right at the table: you can ask the employer to repeat its proposal or say something like, "Let me see if I understand what you are saying." Sometimes silence is a good way to get the other side to repeat itself and give you time to think. Most people do not like silences and will say something to break the quiet. One negotiating expert calls these delays "going to the balcony," that is, pretending that you are on a balcony watching the bargaining below.[23] The distance gives you better perspective.

Union negotiators should always be well prepared for each session, using role-playing beforehand if necessary. On the first day of bargaining, for instance, the union spokesperson could just hand the union's proposed agreement to the employer. But it would be better to hold on to it and make a detailed presentation of what the union wants, complete with supporting documentation. Not only will the employer be forced to sit and listen, but its representatives will also see that the union has prepared its case well. This sends a message to the employer that the union is serious and has probably prepared a sophisticated campaign to secure an agreement. It is not that the union's presentation aims to convince the employer by the force of its logic. The two sides operate on entirely different premises; one side's logic is the other side's illogic. Instead, the union negotiators' skills at the table tell the employer that it can expect a hard struggle from the workers.

A critical element in the bargaining is for the union to know well what is called its "best alternative to a negotiated agreement."[24] The union must know its "resistance point," the point beyond which it would rather not reach agreement, and it must then know what it will do if this point is reached. In negotiations with GM when the CAW was still part of the United Auto Workers, the Canadian union stuck firmly to its position that the workers deserved the annual percentage wage increase which the UAW had first won in the late 1940s. GM insisted on lump-sum wage increases; the workers would get a sum of money each year but their base wage rates would not change. Additional pressure was placed upon the CAW and its chief negotiator, Robert White, by the fact that the U.S. sector of the union had already agreed to lump-sum raises and the UAW leadership badly wanted White to go along. In the face of all of this, White and his staff refused to cave in. Their best alterative to a negotiated agreement was a strike, and they had prepared the membership for it. With all of its Canadian facilities shut down and its U.S. operations' profits threatened, GM relented. The Canadian workers kept their annual percentage wage increases.[25]

The CAW-GM negotiations are an example of *principled* bargaining.[26] The union based its position on a strong union principle, steady increases in real wage rates, and refused to compromise on the principle (though it was willing to make concessions on the amount of the increase). Bargaining based upon principle is difficult to counter, especially if the principle can be framed in terms of fundamental fairness, but that is true only if the principle has strong member support. Some years ago, the union of professional football players in the United States went on strike over the principle of free agency, the right of a player to sell his services to the highest bidder without his current team receiving any compensation from the new team. The union was convinced that this was an issue over which the membership would strike; it based this belief on a poll which it had taken prior to the bargaining. The belief turned out to be erroneous, and not long into the strike the players began to cross their own picket lines and return to work, fearful that they would be permanently replaced. The error of the union was not that the principle was a bad one but that it had not prepared its campaign properly. A poll is no substitute for the comprehensive strategy we have been recommending.

Imaginative bargainers figure out ways to tie issues together so that both sides can win something. (In this regard, it is important to "cost out" all proposals and counter proposals. Today there are computer programs which greatly simplify this.) A friend of mine was negotiating an agreement with a commercial bank after the union had won a rare victory among bank employees. The union had won the representation election by a small margin, and the bank's chief negotiator was using the weakness of support for the union as a weapon to deny the union's demands. The union wanted to secure a *union shop*, an agreement whereby everyone in the bargaining unit had to join the union within a specified number of days. The employer eventually conceded to this demand after the national union promised to deposit a large sum of union money in the bank! In this same negotiation, much of the actual bargaining was done away from the table by the chief negotiators. This is a dangerous tactic because it is done behind the backs of the members. A successful union is one that keeps its members informed of what is going on, so that when the negotiators come back to the members and urge ratification of the contract, the members feel that they were a real part of the bargaining.

What happens if, despite a well-planned contract campaign and good negotiating strategies, the union fails to convince the employer to come to terms? This question needs to be answered in both legal and strategic terms. Under our labor laws, a bargaining stalemate is called an *impasse*. An impasse exists when the NLRB determines that further bargaining is not likely to lead to an agreement. If an impasse does exist, the employer is free to unilaterally impose its last contract offer upon the workers. What usually happens is that the employer declares that the bargaining is at an impasse and imposes its last offer. The union must then file unfair labor practice charges against the employer, accusing it of a violation of Section 8(a)(5) for bargaining in bad faith. It is then up to the NLRB to decide whether or not there is an impasse.

"Negotiations are moving too fast. . . . At this rate we'll reach an agreement with the union in only 10 years!"   (Carol/Simpson)

conducted.[27] This gives the employer an incentive to come to the table with a proposal and refuse to offer any significant modifications. Then when the union digs in and in turn refuses to make concessions, the employer states that the parties are at an impasse, hoping that a compliant board will agree. Labor law scholar Ellen Dannin has argued that the greater ease of employers getting an impasse ruling has led unions to make concessions simply to prevent this from happening.[28] In the past, union negotiators had to avoid language at the table or in the media which suggested that an impasse might exist (such as saying "there is no way we will ever accept" a particular company proposal), but now this may not be enough.

Strategically, the possibility of an impasse should be considered as part of the overall contract campaign and dealt with accordingly. A strike may prove necessary. Employers are more willing to take strikes today than they were when unions had more power. They can and do hire permanent replacements for strikers, and the union-busting consultants know all of the devious tricks to defeat a strike, including using armed thugs. Yet strikes should not be rejected out of hand. The United Mine Workers would never have brought the Pittston out of hand. The United Mine Workers would never have brought the Pittston Coal Company to heel without a strike, including the illegal occupation of one of the struck mines.[29]

A strike is only one way to deal with an impasse, moreover. Some impasses can be resolved through the techniques of *mediation* and *arbitration*. In the private sector of the economy, these devices are voluntary; that is, the parties have to agree to their use. But in the public sector, one or the other is often mandated by law. In mediation, a mediator is brought in to try to get the parties to agree. The mediator will usually meet with each side independently and try to figure out if an agreement is possible, and then begin to float proposals to see how the two sides react; the mediator's proposals may become the basis for a settlement. A union should be very cautious about being completely honest with a mediator; there is no guarantee that the mediator will honor the union's assumption that what it tells the mediator will not be immediately disclosed to the management. A mediator can only recommend contract terms, not impose them. On the other hand, in arbitration, which in this case is called *interest arbitration,* the arbitrator has the power to impose a settlement on the union and the employer. Interest arbitration is very rare in the private sector, but it is sometimes legally required for public employees, especially those who are denied the right to strike. If, for example, the police in a Pennsylvania city cannot reach a settlement with the city's managers, the law requires that a tripartite panel of arbitrators decide what the terms of the contract will be. In a few states, a special kind of interest arbitration, *"final offer" arbitration,* is in force. Once a dispute reaches an impasse, the arbitrator imposes either the union's or the employer's last offer but cannot dictate any sort of compromise solution. It is argued that this will force the parties to negotiate in good faith rather than just going through the motions until arbitration.[30]

THE AGREEMENT

If the union's contract campaign has been successful, the workers and the employer will sign a collective bargaining agreement which will serve as the law of the workplace for its duration. A union should view the contract as a temporary truce agreement.

The contract can be conveniently divided into four parts: union security and management rights, the wage and effort bargain, individual security, and contract administration.[31] A union will try to win in the contract provisions which secure the existence, continuity, and funding of the union; the parts of the agreement which do this are called *union security clauses.* One such clause is a union shop agreement, such as the one negotiated with the bank mentioned above. Another is a dues checkoff provision, in which the employer agrees to deduct union dues from the members' paychecks and remit the money to the union. Such a provision is convenient for the union, but it denies the members a chance to directly confront the union with complaints when the union comes around to collect the dues.[32]

Two important and controversial parts of most agreements today are management rights and no-strike clauses. Nearly all contracts have some sort of *management rights clause,* guaranteeing to the employer certain unilateral rights. The essence of management is control; a good collective bargaining agreement limits this control in significant ways, while a bad one allows the management to retain much of what it already had. Therefore, each part of the agreement should be scrutinized with an eye toward its effect upon managerial control. Some management rights clauses simply state that all matters not specifically dealt with in the agreement become the right of the management. Others spell out in great detail all of the things which the management reserves the right to decide unilaterally. Unions should try to keep management rights as narrowly defined as possible, because the employer will refer to these rights in every dispute with the union over the meaning of the contract. However, even absent a management rights clause, both the NLRB and arbitrators often just assume that certain powers belong to the employer. As corporations continue to downsize, move, and adopt new technology, it will be important for unions to end their longstanding accommodation to the notion that the employer has a right to make all of the fundamental business decisions, while the union limits itself to bargaining over the share of the pie the workers will get.

It is a rare contract which does not have a *no-strike agreement* in it.[33] In such a clause the union agrees not to strike during the duration of the contract; if the union does strike, it opens itself up to a suit under the NLRA and the payment of damages to the employer. The workers who strike in defiance of a no-strike agreement subject themselves to discharge. It has been argued that the no-strike clause is the *quid pro quo* for the employer's acceptance of arbitration to settle contract disputes. Unfortunately in many unions arbitration is a long, drawn-out affair over which the aggrieved worker has little control. The NLRB and arbitrators take the view that a worker should almost always obey a manager's order and then file a grievance if she believes that the order violates the contract. This means that the worker might have a long time to wait before justice is done. With a no-strike clause in effect, direct action by the workers to resolve the dispute is legally prohibited.

Some unions have managed to exempt certain issues from the no-strike agreement. For example, in the automobile industry, the UAW has kept the right to strike over production standards, that is, the amount of work required of any particular job. Similarly, a union might insist on the right to strike over safety issues. In any event, the wording of no-strike clauses is critical. A general no-strike agreement, without any special wording, might be interpreted by the NLRB or the courts to mean that workers cannot refuse to cross another union's picket line, a right which is guaranteed by the law itself even to workers not represented by a union.[34]

The wage and effort bargain could contain literally hundreds of clauses, covering everything from basic wages and benefits to how the workers will be paid (hourly, by the piece, or some combination) to the myriad ways in which the employer seeks to guarantee that the workers will labor with at least some minimal level of intensity. Once the U.S. economy began to slow down and stagnate in the early 1970s, employers became obsessed with raising productivity. One of the outcomes of this was the movement toward various types of labor-management cooperation schemes, in which, in return for granting to the employer greater flexibility in organizing work, the workers were promised greater say in decisionmaking.[35] Thus, many collective bargaining agreements embraced the "team concept." At GM's famous Saturn plant in Tennessee, traditional collective bargaining has disappeared altogether, replaced with a system of joint decisionmaking on a wide variety of issues. The dangers of the team concept are well documented, since they usually weaken the grievance procedure and eliminate hard-won work rules yet never give the union real input into the most fundamental management decisions. Still, the productivity bargaining of the last thirty years does illustrate the great flexibility of collective bargaining. Once the workers have formed a union, the management has to take the workers into account no matter what it does. The nation's shipping companies have been able to introduce labor-saving containerization technology to unload ships, but the unions have forced them to pay a high price for the right to do so.[36] In a nonunion workplace, only the employees pay the price.

Individual security provisions include the grievance procedure and seniority rules. Through the grievance procedure, workers gain fundamental due process, similar to that to which citizens have a right when they come into conflict with the government. The grievance mechanism insures that the members of the bargaining unit are no longer employees "at will." If workers are disciplined "without just cause," they can file grievances. If workers are forced to do work outside of their job classifications, they can file grievances. If the contract has a broad "no discrimination" clause, workers discriminated against by the employer because of some personal characteristic such as race, sex, sexual preference, or political views, can file grievances. Most contracts specify that a grievance is a claim by a member of the bargaining unit that the employer has violated the contract. The worker must file the grievance, usually through the first-level union authority (called a *shop steward*), within the time limit spelled out in the agreement. Then the grievance goes through a series of steps in which successively higher levels of union and management authority try to settle it. If it cannot be settled, the union can insist that a third party, an arbitrator, be brought in to dictate the settlement.

The importance of the grievance procedure cannot be exaggerated. It is what truly separates organized workers from unorganized workers. Its significance can be measured by how rare such a system is in a nonunion company.[37] However, a grievance system is not a substitute for a militant and vigilant rank-and-file controlled union. Grievances should be considered by the union as part of the overall struggle with employers. They should be handled like the bargaining campaign strategy, using education, publicity, solidarity actions, and whatever other tactics best insure victory in grievance resolution. Suppose that a worker is unjustly fired. The union could simply encourage that worker to file a grievance and then process it through the steps, ultimately letting the arbitrator decide whether or not the worker gets reinstated. Or the union could mobilize the membership to act immediately, with information pickets, work-to-rule, in-plant solidarity actions, short stoppages, and the like, as well as filing a formal grievance. The fired worker could be deeply involved in the whole process and not just a passive observer hoping for the right outcome.

Collective bargaining cannot eliminate the uncertainty inherent in our economic system. It cannot prevent plants from closing, and it cannot stop a downturn in the business cycle. However, it can offer workers some job protection through the rule of seniority. Seniority is a powerful union weapon and should be guarded zealously. When my father could no longer breathe well enough to do hard physical labor, his long seniority gave him the right to bid on an easier job. In a nonunion shop, he would simply have been let go. In a layoff, seniority denies the company the power to choose who will go and who will stay. Of course, seniority gives older workers preference over younger ones, but no one stays young forever, and the abuses likely to occur when the employer makes layoff, recall, transfer, and promotion decisions unilaterally far outweigh any discrimination against the young. The fact is that the older we get, the more vulnerable we are; seniority protects us against this vulnerability. Care must be taken to make the seniority provisions of the agreement as strong as possible. For example, employers will insist on getting language which gives it the right to use ability along with seniority in making choices concerning promotions and perhaps layoffs and recalls as well, so the union must make sure that seniority is always the dominant criterion.

One problem which occurs with seniority is that it sometimes perpetuates various forms of discrimination. A plant may be divided into departments, and the contract may grant departmental seniority. A force reduction in Department A might result in the layoff of a person who has worked in the plant for more years than any worker in another department in which there is no reduction. Or a person with a lot of seniority in the plant might transfer into a more desirable department, but this means that his seniority in the new department is zero. A layoff in this new department will result in unemployment for him, while people with less plant seniority but more departmental seniority will remain at work. If the less desirable departments are dominated by racial minorities or women, such a system gives them little incentive to transfer, and this perpetuates the past discrimination which placed them in the inferior departments to begin with. One way to deal with this inequity is to force decisions to be based upon the broadest seniority unit possible, in this case plant seniority. Or layoffs could be allocated in some fixed proportion by race (the least senior white worker is laid off, then the lest senior minority worker, and so forth) until such time as such a system is no longer needed to avoid perpetuating discrimination.[38]

Once a contract is signed, it must be enforced. Again, enforcement should be seen as part of the ongoing campaign to increase the workers' power and should involve all of the members. A union should have democratically elected shop stewards to handle grievances and educate the members, and their powers should be spelled out in the contract. They must be given the contractual right to investigate complaints in the workplace on company time, to have space at work to do this job, to accompany workers to any meetings with supervisors, to meet upon request with managers, to post notices on union bulletin boards in the workplace, and to request and obtain all information needed to accomplish their tasks in an efficient and timely manner. Some of these rights are guaranteed by the labor laws, but they will be that much stronger if protected by the contract as well.[39]

Arbitration of contract disputes is such an important part of collective bargaining that it deserves some specific commentary.[40] As opposed to interest arbitration (in which the arbitrator decides the terms of the contract itself), in this type of dispute resolution, called *grievance arbitration,* the arbitrator decides whether or not the employer has violated an already existing agreement. Once the last internal step of the grievance procedure has failed to generate a settlement of the grievance, the union has so many days to invoke arbitration. This done, the contract will specify how the arbitrator is to be selected. A few contracts provide for permanent arbitrators who will arbitrate all of the grievances which arise, but most contracts make each arbitration ad hoc. Anyone can be selected as an arbitrator; there are no specific qualifications which a person must have to be one. Naturally the parties will be wise to choose someone well versed in collective bargaining agreements. There are national associations of arbitrators, the best known of which is the American Arbitration Association. Some states maintain panels of arbitrators as well. Any of these organizations will send a list of arbitrators to the parties upon request, and this is something which may be included in the contract. Among public employees and employers in Pennsylvania, a common procedure is to request a list of arbitrators from the state's panel of arbitrators maintained by the Bureau of Mediation in Harrisburg, the state capitol. Upon receipt of the arbitrator list, the union and the employer will successively eliminate arbitrators until one is left. This person will be notified that he or she has been selected by the parties. The chosen arbitrator will then work out a date for an arbitration hearing which accommodates both sides. Unions should keep track of arbitration decisions, some of which are published and most of which are sent to the appropriate association or bureau. These rulings can give the union some idea of how it might fare with a particular arbitrator.

An arbitration hearing is a quasi-legal proceeding. Both the union and the employer will make opening statements, often through an attorney (union staff can learn to do this, though often lawyers are best suited for it); both sides will present their cases through witnesses, who will be both examined and cross-examined; both sides will introduce documents as evidence (such as the collective bargaining agreement, negotiations notes, management memoranda, etc.); and both parties may be requested by the arbitrator to write closing briefs, in which they are free to cite prior arbitration decisions for the use of the arbitrator. Formal rules of law, such as a prohibition of hearsay evidence, usually apply, although somewhat more loosely than in a court of law. Witnesses are sworn in and can be subpoenaed to appear by the arbitrator. After the hearing is closed, the arbitrator reads the briefs and notes from the hearing and examines all of the evidence, then makes a ruling which is binding on the union and on the management. Numerous court decisions have made it very difficult for the losing side to overturn an arbitrator's ruling.

Unions should prepare for arbitration as they do for bargaining, involving the grievant or grievants at every step. The shop steward should carefully investigate the grievance and seek out any and all evidence which might buttress the case at arbitration. The employer is legally bound to give the union any information it has that might be relevant to the case, such as, for example, attendance and discipline records. If possible, witnesses should be secured who will corroborate the grievant's claims. Role-playing should be used to prepare workers to give testimony and to face what might be nasty cross-examination. The collective bargaining agreement should be scoured for provisions supportive of the union's arguments. In other words, the preparation for arbitration should be an exercise in solidarity-building.

The arbitrator normally goes into an arbitration cold, with only the most general idea of the nature of the grievance. Therefore, it is incumbent upon the union to make the issue as clear as possible as soon as possible. The arbitrator's first obligation is to make a ruling faithful to the collective bargaining agreement, so the contract is often the most important piece of evidence presented. Crucial is any testimony telling the arbitrator what a particular provision means, what the parties intended it to mean, or how it has been interpreted in the past. If the contract is vague or silent on an issue, the past practices of the parties are important. And in some cases the arbitrator will just try to do what is fair; for example, an arbitrator may decide whether a work rule is fair to a rational person or may determine that the employer's discipline was too harsh for the offense. Knowledge of what arbitrators do when they make rulings is useful to the union in preparing its case.

Employers and outsiders often say the a union will take any case to arbitration, even that of a worker who deserves discharge, such as someone who is chronically drunk at work. Such an argument cannot be taken seriously. First of all, a grievance procedure is a due process clause, and, as in courts of law, every person has the right to due process, with a presumption of innocence. Second, a union has a legal obligation to investigate thoroughly every grievance, irrespective of the character of the grievant or the nature of the grievance. A union does not have to push every grievance to arbitration, but it could risk a lawsuit by the worker if it does not take a particular complaint to arbitration.[41] Finally, there may be times when it is wise, in terms of building solidarity, to take even a weak grievance to arbitration, to show the membership that the union is militantly fighting for their rights.

POLITICS AND COLLECTIVE BARGAINING

Scholars of our labor movement have often argued that two tendencies have marked the struggle to build unions. On the one hand, there have been overtly political workers' groups, such as the Knights of Labor, the Socialists, and the Communists. The aim of these organizations has been to directly confront the economic system and the state which supports it, with the goal of establishing a more egalitarian society without a wage system. Such movements were not particularly interested in collective bargaining per se, or if they were, unions affiliated with such movements did not see it in the same way as more conservative unions. On the other hand, there were movements of working people which had no particular political platform and simply concentrated on organizing unions to bargain for better wages, hours, and terms and conditions of employment. The most important of these organizations was the American Federation of Labor, whose founder, Samuel Gompers, urged workers to reject radical politics and operate within the two-party system of Republicans and Democrats.

Many scholars who are themselves radicals reject collective bargaining as inherently conservative (much as did the IWW), as essentially an ingenious device through which union bureaucrats and their managerial counterparts can contain and routinize worker-employer conflict.[42] Collective bargaining, by its nature, accepts the rights of the employers to run their businesses and relegates the workers to winning a slightly bigger share of the pie than they could without a union. In this view, collective bargaining, along with legislation like the NLRA which promotes it, is a trick played on workers to prevent them from taking more radical actions on their own behalf.

Recent studies by Maurice Zeitlin and Judith Stepan-Norris rebut this view.[43] What matters in collective bargaining (and by extension in union organizing and contract campaigns) is the context in which it occurs. Zeitlin and Stepan-Norris compared contracts secured by left-wing, centrist, and right-wing unions between the years 1937 and 1955 (1955 was the year of the merger of the AFL and the CIO). All of the unions were affiliated with the CIO. The left-wing unions, those most closely allied with the Communist Party and radical politics, won contracts which best enabled workers to protect their interests and build a basis for further victories against the employers.

Specifically, the left-led unions were far more likely to have negotiated collective bargaining agreements with either no or weak management rights clauses, without no-strike agreements, with short durations (so that when contracts did include a no-strike agreement, it would not hamstring the workers for very long), and with worker-friendly grievance procedures (union representative present at first step, relatively few steps, and strict time limits for each step). Unions which espoused a more conservative philosophy, such as labor-management cooperation, won agreements clearly weaker in each of these areas. Unions which won better contracts also were usually the most democratic and subject to rank-and-file control. The lesson to be taken from these studies is that the most effective labor movement is one that has radical, democratic principles and acts upon them.

Through collective bargaining, workers have fought for and won impressive improvements in their standard of living, measured not just in monetary terms but in terms of human dignity. Mine workers have won both the right to be paid from the time they enter the mine until they leave it and washrooms to clean themselves before they leave; steel workers have won generous early retirement benefits; teachers have gained some control over what they teach and the size of their classes; nurses have won limitations on the number of patients for whom they are responsible; janitors have won an end to the subcontracting of their work; and all union workers have won the right to stand up to the employer with dignity and without fear. While employers have condemned unions and collective bargaining as detrimental to managerial flexibility, workers have used them to deal creatively with disparate and rapidly changing circumstances. Today, some agreements provide childcare facilities in the workplace, flexible work schedules, transfer rights, limitations upon overtime, prohibitions against sexual harassment, sabbatical leaves, retraining and education funds, affirmative action, and a host of other innovative procedures and programs. Yet it must be said that collective bargaining cannot alone emancipate working people from those aspects of life which are part and parcel of an economic system like ours. It cannot guarantee employment or meaningful work, or a clean environment, or an end to racism and sexism. Unions and collective bargaining are only a part of what working people must build for themselves on the way to a better society.

CHAPTER FIVE

UNIONS AND POLITICS: LOCAL, NATIONAL, GLOBAL

Unions are vehicles by which workers can secure a voice in many workplace decisions and at the same time obtain higher compensation for their labors. However, there are some concerns that working people cannot adequately address through struggles at their places of employment. An economic system such as ours seldom generates enough employment to go around. Those few who own most of our workplaces have taken great pains to economize on the use of labor and to maximize the number of people who can do any given job. They have done this in a variety of ways, from dividing up jobs so that little skilled labor is needed to replacing workers with machines and transporting capital around the globe. The effect of these actions is to create a "reserve army of labor," a pool of potential workers whose function it is to reduce the wages (lowering the price of labor by increasing the "supply") and increase the insecurity of those who are currently employed. The problem of unemployment, therefore, is systemic (brought about by the nature of capitalism), and all but impossible to deal with in collective bargaining. It must be confronted at the level of society as a whole.[1]

Social problems require social action. Many companies produce products or use technology which do great damage to workers' health and the environment. Asbestos workers not only died a little each day at work, but the product they produced harmed people around the world.[2] These problems might be partially dealt with by a union, which can force a company to use safer equipment and reduce the exposure of the workers to toxic materials.[3] But a union will be an inadequate vehicle for addressing widespread environmental destruction. What is more, there will be situations in which workers will be torn between their desire for a better environment and their need for adequate employment. Automobiles do great harm to our health and safety (air pollution, acid rain, congestion, noise, accidents), but it would be foolish to expect the automobile workers' union to solve this problem if doing so meant that their members would face unemployment. Likewise, consider health care. Unions have won good health benefits for their members, but the level of benefits won exhibits a good deal of variability among different groups of workers. Most workers in the United States do not enjoy union representation and, therefore, they may have no health insurance at all.[4] Yet from a human rights standpoint, it is essential that all workers have the same minimum level of benefits.

Consider finally what we might call the institutional framework in which unions are formed and bargaining takes place. All capitalist societies have complex legal systems, which have considerable bearing on the relationship between workers and their employers. For example, until the late 1950s it was typically held in the United States that public employees (who now comprise nearly 20 percent of the workforce) could join unions, but they could not compel their employers to negotiate with them. In addition, it was illegal for them to strike, making it legal for their employers to fire them if they did. No public employees' union could change these circumstances. What was required was a change in the laws.[5]

Employers, while in ruthless competition with one another, are well organized to protect the interests of their entire class. Sometimes this takes the form of purely private actions, as when a group of employers agrees to provide money to a single employer in their industry so that this employer can withstand a strike. But much more common is the political collaboration of employers. While the government of a capitalist economy such as ours is formally independent of the economy, in practice it is intimately connected. Politicians need money to get elected, and governments need money to function. Those who own the wealth and have most of the income are in a pivotal position to influence what the government does, both by providing money for

Health care workers from New York's Local 1199 at the AFL-CIO's 1991 Solidarity Day rally, Washington, D.C. (Jim West)

electoral campaigns and in taxes and by being major buyers of the bonds which governments often sell to pay their bills. Under circumstances in which workers are poorly organized, it is a certainty that the government will, for the most part, do the bidding of the employers.

It is often difficult to know where business stops and government begins.[6] Who hasn't heard the slogans, "The business of America is business," and "What's good for General Motors is good for the country"? There are literally scores of cases in which the federal government used the armed forces to defeat strikes.[7] The federal government gave millions of dollars and millions of acres to the big railroad companies and then sent Eugene V. Debs to jail for having the temerity to challenge their power. The entire legal machinery, from the laws to the courts, was stacked against working people from the earliest days of the republic until the 1930s. Individual labor unions sometimes achieved great things for their members, but they were powerless in the face of the collective power of business expressed in the armed might of the government.

WHY U.S. LABOR POLITICS ARE DIFFERENT

From the beginning, working men and women were not ignorant of the political power of the capitalist class. They sought ways to limit and challenge it. This was the case in western Europe as well, but the situation there was somewhat different than in the United States. European nations had long had authoritarian political systems, with the central government firmly integrated into the economic system. When workers began to organize unions, they came into immediate conflict with the government, and it appeared to many labor leaders and intellectuals that the only way for working people to advance was to capture control of the state. During England's industrial revolution at the end of the eighteenth century, for example, not only did workers *not* have the right to vote, but they also faced time in prison if they formed a labor union. Therefore, workers were quick to form labor political organizations and parties which had the aim of capturing control of the government. These political parties were, generally speaking, hostile to capitalism itself; they set out to establish a cooperative economic system which would not rely on a labor market and wages.[8] The politics of these parties can thus be described as socialist or communist. Two of capitalism's greatest critics, Karl Marx and Friedrich Engels, were influential advisors and participants in the development of working-class political organizations and labor parties throughout most of their adult lives.[9]

In the United States, circumstances did not favor the formation of radical labor parties.[10] Here white men and to some extent white women formed a nation by revolting against the English monarchy. They established what was, for its time, a radically democratic society. To the extent that most white working men saw the government as theirs as much as the merchants' and factory owners', they did not undertake to form a labor party.[11] When some of them did try, they found that the two-party system was so firmly entrenched and sanctioned by the laws that it was hard to mount a third-party challenge. The major parties often coopted the workers' best leaders, further weakening their independent political efforts. The racist legacy of slavery propelled many workers into alliance with their white employers in politics, blocking common cause with the black working class.[12] Finally, the ideology of individualism and competition was stronger in the United States than anywhere else in the world, making workers skeptical of radical working-class politics and making it easy for employers to portray such politics as the work of foreigners.[13] This ideology was on every point supported by the police power of the government, which turned a wrathful eye on any sort of labor radicalism, whether in politics or the unions.

Despite these many obstacles to independent labor politics (a political expression of the labor movement), labor political organizations and parties did form, not much different from their counterparts in Europe and often led by recently arrived European immigrant workers. Parties such as the Socialist Labor Party, the Socialist Party, and the Communist Party formed as capitalism in the United States took on its modern form in the late nineteenth and early twentieth centuries. These all gained followings among workers, and at various times they had considerable influence within the labor unions, especially the Socialist Party before the First World War and the Communist Party during the Great Depression and the 1940s. However, none of them was able to challenge the political dominance of the Republican and Democratic parties, both of which were dominated by big business interests. Radical parties were hounded and harassed by employers and by the government, and not a few of their leaders were sent to prison for upholding their beliefs.[14]

Some labor leaders, most notably Samuel Gompers and the other founders of the American Federation of Labor, argued that the best course for workers in the United States was to abandon labor politics and concentrate on building strong labor unions. Gompers observed that craft unions could take advantage of the employers' dependence upon the workers' skills to win admirable wages, hours, and working conditions. The labor parties wanted a legally mandated eight-hour day, but some craft unions had already won this through the economic pressures they could place upon recalcitrant employers. Craft unions were made up of white men, often of the same ethnicity, and this made it easier for them to act collectively. But even among them, Gompers observed, politics was often a divisive subject, which if placed at the forefront of the labor movement would make most collective struggles impossible to sustain.[15]

Gompers's solution to the problem of politics was to accept the status quo of the two-party system. The craft unions would use the strength of their economic pressure and their numbers to make politicians act in the interests of labor. As he put it, labor should "reward its friends and punish its enemies," whether they be Republicans or Democrats. Such a "pragmatic" politics would avoid the divisiveness of a labor politics and, at the same time, would not bring down the wrath of the government upon the house of labor. Unions would act as lobbying groups for pro-labor candidates and pro-labor public policies. However, not too much faith was put in government by the AFL. So often had the government betrayed labor that Gompers had little hope that the salvation of workers could be achieved politically. Instead workers would organize into unions and through their unions get what they needed.

Over the years the AFL's "anti-politics" politics hardened into a conservative ideology.[16] Craft unions, in cities in which they had a strong presence, developed cozy relationships with the politicians who could throw work their members' way, but this involved a great deal of corruption between union officials, business owners, and local public officials. These unions were never very democratic internally and occasionally some of them were taken over by criminal elements.[17] At the national level, the AFL did fight for protective federal laws, especially one law which would free unions from the grip of deadly labor injunctions. But bereft of a perspective that comprehended the basic conflict of interest between workers and employers, the AFL was unable to build a political movement that could compel the government to act in the interests of working people. By the early 1930s, the AFL had actually come out against much needed government programs such as unemployment compensation, arguing that if workers got these things through the government they would lose interest in the unions and would give up their independence.

LABOR POLITICS IN THE 1930s

The upheaval which spawned the CIO during the 1930s also changed the politics of organized labor. Future CIO leaders like John L. Lewis fought hard for federal legislation, and these efforts paid off with the passage of the National Labor Relations Act in 1935, the year of the CIO's birth. In addition, this period marked the heyday of radical organizations like the Communist Party, which was to one degree or another in favor of an independent labor party (though, of course, the Communists wanted this party to be their party). The radical self-organization of workers in basic industries, and the alienation felt by many

workers toward the economic system and the government, created the precon-
ditions for a labor party.[18]

However, in the end, independent labor politics did not win out during the
Great Depression. Most of the leaders of the CIO unions had come to maturity
within the milieu of AFL pragmatism and could not, even in the crucible of
Great Depression radicalism, bring themselves to champion a labor party.
Lewis probably came the closest to a full break with the two-party status quo.
In the 1936 presidential elections, Lewis practically emptied the treasury of the
United Mine Workers to support Franklin Roosevelt's reelection and Demo-
crats in Congress. When Roosevelt moved toward the right after the election,
Lewis broke with him. But Lewis had been a lifelong Republican. He simply did
not have the radical outlook required to see the necessity of forming a working
class party.[19]

Furthermore, the national Democratic Party, under the leadership of
Roosevelt, saw the new unions as the basis for the renewal and long-term power
of the party. The working masses, many of them voting for the first time, swept
the Democrats into office in 1932 and 1936. To insure that this continued to
happen, Roosevelt began to curry the favor of the more conservative and pliable
CIO leaders. Roosevelt shunned the independent Lewis and had nothing to do
with the truly radical CIO leaders, but he praised men like Sidney Hillman of the
clothing workers and Philip Murray of the steel workers. The president's approval
helped these leaders to consolidate their positions within the labor movement, and
they then used their power to tie the unions to the Democratic Party.

The Second World War consolidated the union-Democrat alliance. The War
Labor Board, established to deal with labor disputes, wage increases, and
strikes, brought conservative labor leaders on board. Hillman and the other
board members from labor began to meet with their capitalist counterparts to
plan labor's role in the war effort, and this more or less completed the co-optation of labor into the Democratic Party. Labor leaders believed that they were
sharing power with big business, and that they had great influence inside of the
government. But this alliance was based upon the absence of a mass movement
of workers and democratic unionism. Instead, decisions were made at the top,
and member apathy and obedience were encouraged. After the war, the CIO
unions were split between those who had allied with the Democratic Party and

the radicals who wanted greater political independence. The former, aided by the government and by their presumed class enemy, destroyed the radicals. This was made easier because some of these radicals were in the milieu of the Communist Party, which became a target of repressive government policies when the Cold War began in the late 1940s. The consequence was that all of labor was greatly weakened. Unions had some say within the Democratic Party, but they were very much junior partners to business, which, understanding that labor could not fight as strongly as before, began to lay the groundwork for the full-blown attack on organized labor that was to commence in the early 1970s.[20]

THE AFL-CIO AND POLITICS TODAY

The AFL had always been more conservative than the CIO and had actually urged Congress to investigate the NLRB, which it alleged favored the CIO. This position put it firmly on the side of the employers, who had the same view. But the politics of the AFL and the CIO converged after the defeat of the radicals in the CIO in the 1940s. In 1955, the two organizations merged and continued to practice a modern version of the pragmatic politics of Samuel Gompers. Let us look at some examples of labor politics to see exactly how this has worked.

First, it is important to note that labor politics has operated at local, national, and international levels. Unions which depend upon local political decisions continue the tradition of maintaining close ties with local politicians. In Pittsburgh, for example, the local construction unions, who are still quite powerful, recently worked out a labor-management accord through the offices of the county commissioners. They agreed not to strike during the construction of a new airport in return for an agreement that union labor would be used for the work. Municipal employees' unions naturally try to build alliances with local politicians, because these will ultimately set the budgets out of which wages will be paid. In most localities, the central labor councils (CLCs) act as the hub of local labor political activity. Traditionally, this has meant that the local council will lobby local government on behalf of union programs and get out the vote for labor's candidates at election time. CLC unions will get members to circulate petitions for candidates, contribute money, do leafletting and door-to-door canvassing, and operate phone banks during the days preceding an election. In these ways, labor hopes to get its candidates elected and to get officials, once in office, to support labor's agenda. Usually, though not always, the closest ties are to Democrats.

In general, political policy is set by the AFL-CIO's national leadership and filters down to lower administrative levels.[21] Of course, the AFL-CIO does not set the policies of the national unions, which, though affiliated with the AFL-CIO, are autonomous entities with their own policy-making structures. The United Auto Workers, for example, has its own political agenda, and it has not always accorded with that of the AFL-CIO. The UAW even has its own international affairs department, reflecting the fact that the automobile industry operates on a global scale. National unions might have their own Political Action Committees (PACs), and these may support policies or politicians different from those supported by the AFL-CIO's PAC, the Committee on Political Education (COPE). Generalizations about labor's politics do not, therefore, necessarily describe the politics of all unions. This is especially true of some independent unions. The United Electrical Workers have maintained a political stance far to the left of the AFL-CIO, for many years favoring the formation of an independent labor party.

The politics of the AFL-CIO is established by the federation's officers, none of whom are elected directly by union members. The chief officers are elected by delegates to the AFL-CIO's biennial convention, as are the members of the executive board, which typically consists of the presidents of the most powerful national unions. The delegates to the convention are selected by the national unions, which may or may not mean that they were elected by the memberships of the unions. To a considerable extent, the policies which the AFL-CIO supports and tries to get made into law or public policy reflect the needs of working people. Thus the national AFL-CIO has always championed such things as increases in the minimum wage and more comprehensive guarantees of health insurance for all workers.[22] And it has at least given lip service to full civil rights for racial and ethnic minorities and women. It has strongly supported better labor laws: it pushed for labor-friendly reforms to the NLRA and for the enactment of the Occupational Safety and Health Act. It has fought for laws providing for union scale wages for workers on projects funded by the federal government, for pension reform so that workers could not be arbitrarily stripped of their pension benefits, and for legislation extending the right to unionize and bargain collectively to public employees. Recently it has struggled to win passage of a law prohibiting employers from permanently replacing strikers and for the defeat of the North American Free Trade Agreement.[23] It actively rejected the Republican Party's anti-social service Contract with America, and its research department developed good materials which exposed the bogus statistics and analysis upon which the Contract was based.[24]

The problem is not so much the nature of the policies which the AFL-CIO favors, although those could be more far-reaching. The difficulty has been in the political strategy and structure of the organization, which have made it increasingly difficult for labor to get what it wants politically. The AFL-CIO has relied far too heavily upon a staff of paid lobbyists in Washington, D.C. These lobbyists, reflecting the overall political philosophy of the AFL-CIO, spend their time currying favor with Democratic Party politicians and operatives in the traditional "you scratch my back and I'll scratch yours" style. This has not worked especially well, both because the Democratic Party is not really the party of labor and because the AFL-CIO has seldom mobilized rank-and-file workers to put heat on the politicians. Consider some representative examples:

• In 1976, labor strongly endorsed the Carter/Mondale ticket. Jimmy Carter, from the right-to-work state of Georgia, had never shown much sympathy for organized labor, but Mondale was from a labor stronghold, Minnesota, and was a long-time friend of organized labor. During the first two years of this administration, the AFL-CIO pushed hard for some mild pro-labor reforms of the National Labor Relations Act.[25] Among the reform bill's provisions were expedited certification election procedures, monetary penalties for employer refusal to bargain, and stronger penalties for certain other employer unfair labor practices. Both houses of Congress were controlled by Democrats, many of whom had been actively supported by labor, and the president was a Democrat and on record as supporting the bill. Nevertheless, the bill never got out of the Senate, the victim of a filibuster. President Carter never used his considerable arm-twisting powers to get the bill passed, and the same was true for many other powerful Democrats. In addition, the AFL-CIO never bothered to educate its members about the bill's significance, nor did it build a mobilization campaign to rally member support and action. Employers, on the other hand, went all-out to defeat the bill. Employer-funded organizations had members send millions of postcards and letters to Congressional representatives demanding that they vote against the reforms. Scores of plant managers were flown into Washington to meet with their representatives and senators and to testify before the relevant committees. Without counter-pressure from voting workers, the legislators simply did not see it in their career interests to rally around the bill.

• In 1996, the AFL-CIO once again warmly endorsed a Democrat for president, this time Bill Clinton. Before he had become the frontrunner for the Democratic Party nomination in 1992, Clinton had little labor support. He was the governor of one of the nation's poorest and most anti-union states, and was financed by the state's largest and worst employers, including chicken processors like Tyson, whose workers are among the country's most exploited.[26] I remember teaching a group of automobile workers at that time; they were uniformly hostile to Clinton. One man said that as you crossed the Mississippi River from Memphis into Arkansas, all that you saw were miles and miles of shacks. Yet once Clinton was sure to be nominated, the organized labor officialdom gave him its unconditional support. His first term was a monumental disappointment to working people. Although he did appoint a relatively decent man, Robert Reich, to head the Department of Labor, all of his other appointees were drawn from the corporate elite and their hirelings. Clinton offered only the most tepid support for the banning of permanent striker replacements, forming instead a commission to promote labor-management cooperation and the elimination of the legal prohibition of company unions. Not once did he mention raising the badly eroded minimum wage during the early part of his first term, when the Democrats still controlled the House of Representatives.[27]

Not only that, but Clinton aggressively promoted the interests of the wealthy. He embraced the anti-labor policies of Alan Greenspan, chairman of the Board of Governors of the Federal Reserve System. And he pulled out all of the stops to get the North American Free Trade Agreement (NAFTA) enacted into law. Most unions bitterly opposed NAFTA, understanding correctly that it threatened decent-paying jobs in the United States. NAFTA encourages companies to move operations to the low-wage Mexican economy, while at the same time it makes it very difficult for any of the three countries it covers (Mexico, the United States, and Canada) to legislate controls over the movement of capital and products across borders.[28] To their credit, the AFL-CIO and many member unions did mount a good campaign against NAFTA, with numerous grassroots actions, not only among U.S. workers but among workers in all three countries. Despite massive corporate and government propaganda in favor of NAFTA, the general public continued to oppose it. Then Clinton went to work, putting maximum pressure on undecided Democrats and promising support for their pet projects. Tens of millions of dollars were promised in exchange for support for the treaty, and in the end, the politicians caved in and voted for NAFTA.[29]

You might think that Clinton's promotion of NAFTA would have chilled labor support for him. But such was not the case. The new leadership of the AFL-CIO endorsed Clinton well before the Democratic convention, and then spent more than $30 million to get him and other Democrats elected. This endorsement took place in the face of Clinton's support for the dismantling of the welfare system, the long-term effect of which will be the destitution of millions of working families, single women, and children. Neither the Democratic Party nor President Clinton made any commitments to labor in return for union campaign dollars. And since winning reelection, Clinton has done nothing to champion labor's causes, even refusing to appoint anyone moderately pro-labor to chair the Department of Labor. (Secretary Reich resigned, making some muted allusions to his boss's capitulation to the rich and powerful.)[30]

A second difficulty with the AFL-CIO's political structure is that the federation has never put forward a clearly working-class perspective. The employing class will make concessions to workers, but only if workers are organized enough to force the employers' hand. With the co-optation of much of the CIO's leadership and the eventual ejection of the more radical and independent elements from the labor movement, pragmatic politics became the handmaiden to those who really controlled the Democratic Party. No doubt, those co-opted began to feel that their credibility and respectability depended upon their acceptability to these same rulers. This meant that the AFL-CIO could not

(Mike Konopaki)

even think of mobilizing the masses of workers for anything which the leaders of the Democratic Party found unacceptable. This capitulation was sometimes defended on the grounds that it was better to get a few crumbs than nothing at all, but all too often it has been nothing at all which workers have gotten. Under these circumstances, a politics of pragmatism was bound to degenerate into a politics of class collaboration. Both of the major political parties are dominated by money and the ultimate "special interest," corporate capital; even the Democratic Party, which receives most union contributions, gets far more of its funding from corporations and corporate lawyers.[31]

Even those working people who lack a sophisticated understanding of politics know that the Democrats have failed to deliver much in the way of tangible improvements in working-class living standards or increased democracy. Seeing their union leaders cozying up to politicians who are far removed from the experiences of working people has often left members disgusted and unwilling to follow union endorsements at election time. Thus we had the incredible irony of workers voting in large numbers for Ronald Reagan, whose politics favored the rich, damaged unions, and drove down the wages of America's working-class majority.[32] To those voters, the right wing at least seemed to stand for something, to be emotionally committed to core values.

What was missing from the labor movement was a philosophy to which people might be willing to make sacrifices in order to see it become a reality. Such a philosophy must be, without apology, a class philosophy, one which recognizes the position of workers in this system—a system which, by its very nature, puts them in fundamental opposition to their employers. It must teach that the only real hope for working people lies in collective organization, not just to improve their circumstances within our economic system but to create the conditions in which the things workers now have to fight for are taken for granted as basic human rights.

THE MISSOURI VICTORY AGAINST RIGHT-TO-WORK[33]

A *"right-to-work" law* is a state statute which makes it illegal for a union and an employer to negotiate either a union shop or an agency shop. When a union organizes a shop in a right-to-work state, it cannot compel members of the bargaining unit to pay dues or a dues equivalent, despite the fact that those who do not join the union receive all of the contract benefits which the union wins in bargaining. These laws allow the employer to play off those who are in the union against those who are not and to selectively hire union opponents with the hope of eventually getting them to decertify the union. There are twenty right-to-work states, mostly in the South. Studies have shown that workers in right-to-work states are worse off in terms of a variety of economic and social indicators, and that a right-to-work law causes union membership to be lower than it would otherwise be.[34]

In 1977, right-to-work supporters, led by the National Right to Work Committee (a right-wing organization founded in 1954 and funded mostly by corporations), successfully petitioned to get a proposed state constitutional amendment on the Missouri ballot. Just four months before the election, polls indicated that two-thirds of voters supported the right-to-work amendment, including 40 percent of all union voters. The state's labor movement, badly fragmented and reliant on the AFL-CIO lobbying model, seemed about to be dealt a terrible defeat. Yet labor managed in this short time to rally voters into opposition to right-to-work and soundly defeated the amendment. The unions did this by organizing and mobilizing the members.

A three-prong strategy was developed, with maximum involvement by workers in each part. First, the union launched a voter registration drive, with a focus on union members and those identified as likely to vote against the amendment. Rank-and-file workers were energized to make multiple contacts, through phone banks and home visits, and in the end, 366,000 people were contacted, 24,000 volunteers were recruited, and 190,000 new voters registered. One hundred thousand more votes were cast on the amendment than in the political races. Every group targeted, except college students, voted against right-to-work. Second, a massive media campaign was launched, with "Right to Work is a Ripoff" as the slogan. All told, the media group put together by the campaign did one hundred separate jobs and generated nearly nine million pieces of literature. Third, coalitions with other groups were built. It was discovered that most groups had a stake in a high wage economy, exactly what right-to-work could not produce. Small farmers were contacted; they came to oppose right-to-work because they hire few workers and depend on decent wages to sell their crops locally. Similarly, African Americans were solidly opposed, because more than any other group, black workers depended on a high wage labor market. Consumer, environmental, anti-nuclear, and religious groups were also brought into the fold. All in all, it was a textbook campaign. It is too bad that labor nationally did not learn this Missouri lesson: mobilize, build coalitions, act decisively. If it had, perhaps the debacle of the 1980s would not have happened.

WORKERS OF THE WORLD SUPPRESSED

Labor politics in the United States also has an international dimension, one which has been the source of much controversy.[35] The early AFL was strongly chauvinistic, even to the point of urging Congress to legislate restrictions on the immigration of certain groups into the United States. It is painful to read the vitriolic anti-Chinese comments of Samuel Gompers and virtually every other AFL leader. Of course, to a great extent, this was but a reflection of the racism which marked much of American culture. Even many radical union leaders were racist in practice.

In its very early years, the AFL maintained a position of pacifism, and in its 1898 and 1899 conventions it came out strongly against rising U.S. imperialism. This view was much contested during the so-called Spanish-American War, in which the United States annexed Cuba, Puerto Rico, and the Phillippines, after suppressing their independence movements. But the AFL soon began to actively support U.S. imperialism. During and after the First World War, the AFL became fanatical in its support of U.S. foreign policy, especially its anticommunism. It fully supported the numerous U.S. interventions abroad before the Second World War, such as those in Cuba, Panama, Haiti, and Nicaragua. It seldom raised a complaint against the government's war on radical labor organizations such as the IWW and those with close ties to the Socialist and Communist parties. It accepted the government's argument that these organizations were anti-American and usually controlled by foreign powers.[36]

The radicals who were so important in the union drives of the Great Depression included many types: socialists, followers of the revolutionary Marxist Leon Trotsky, activists in A. J. Muste's American Workers Party, and idealistic adherents of various other currents. A very high percentage were members of or close to the Communist Party. After the Second World War, these radicals were, as we have seen, driven out of the mainstream of the labor movement, accused of being dupes of the Soviet Union and tools of the Soviet dictator Joseph Stalin. As critics from the right and left have charged, the U.S. Communist Party was controlled in fundamental ways by the ruling Communist Party of the Soviet Union, a relationship which sometimes damaged its work in the labor movement. However, it did not follow from this that Communists in the labor movement were simply tools of Stalin, continually sacrificing American trade unionists' well-being on the altar of Communism. Despite their flaws, their expulsion from the labor movement was a tragedy with far-reaching consequences, detrimental to the whole of labor, not just the American left. It is no accident that after the purge of the radicals, the U.S. labor movement's international politics became increasingly indistinguishable from the politics of the U.S. State Department.

Globally, the period after the Second World War was one of revolutionary upheaval. In the immediate aftermath of the war, left-wing movements were poised to take power in Greece and Italy. The Communists were winning the civil war, which had raged in China since 1926. The Vietnamese Communists were defeating the French colonialists and would deal them the decisive blow in 1954. The Soviet Union was establishing satellite states in Eastern Europe. A little later the spark of revolution ignited in Africa and Latin America.

The U.S. government had begun to formulate a strategy to defeat revolution before the war was over, and as soon as it was ended began to implement the policies summed up in the phrase, "Cold War."[37] Significantly, one part of the Cold War was the use of the U.S. labor movement to block the formation of radical labor movements around the world. Much of the co-optation of labor was done through its close alliance with the Democratic Party. The International Affairs Department of the merged AFL-CIO became a haven for fanatical cold warriors, including a number of former Communists. Several unions became conduits for monies sent by the CIA to foreign countries to subvert any labor movement which dared to defy the imperial policies of the U.S. government. Eventually entities affiliated with the AFL-CIO but largely funded by the CIA and later by the State Department were established to formalize and bureaucratize the collaboration between the U.S. government and the labor movement.

Despite the generally reactionary international position of the AFL and the AFL-CIO, many unions and union members have held and acted upon more progressive views. In addition to the AFL's early pacifism and the widespread labor opposition to the First World War, the CIO was originally hostile to U.S. imperialism and opposed the initiation of the Cold War. The left-led unions expelled from the CIO which were able to survive continued in their steadfast support of international worker solidarity. The Vietnam war eventually fostered renewed opposition to war (and sometimes also to empire) within labor, although the AFL-CIO leadership, especially Federation President George Meany, for the most part supported that immoral war to the end. Nixon's escalation of the war into Cambodia and the murder of students at Kent State and Jackson State brought millions of union members to support troop withdrawal, in conflict with labor's top leaders. In addition, the anti-war movement of the 1960s radicalized thousands of young people, some of whom found their way into the labor movement, where many have remained to this day.

The internal struggle of the labor movement over foreign policy intensified during the 1980s as the U.S. government waged war against the workers and peasants of Central America. So too did the struggle within many unions and in the AFL-CIO over the decline of the labor movement and the lack of democracy in the house of labor. Meany's successor, Lane Kirkland, continued the Cold War program of the AFL-CIO, but the hold of knee-jerk anticommunism over the labor movement was weakening. Support for Central American police states seemed inexcusable in light of the growing passivity of labor union leadership in the face of open corporate warfare. The collapse of working-class living standards over a generation pointed more than ever to the need for unionization, but the labor movement was not rising to the task. As the Reagan/Bush years ended, the rumbling of dissidents in the labor movement grew louder, and in 1995, new and more progressive leaders wrested control from the old guard. Fortunately, the new leadership in the AFL-CIO appears to have begun to dismantle the old International Affairs Department and to reorient the new one toward real solidarity with the world's millions of oppressed workers.

THE AMERICAN INSTITUTE
FOR FREE LABOR DEVELOPMENT

For well over one hundred years, the United States has acted as if it were entitled to exploit the economies of Latin America and intervene in the internal affairs of that region whenever it desired. This policy, known as the Monroe Doctrine, has led to actions which have caused the death of hundreds of thousands of workers and peasants in countries from Mexico to Chile.[38] Unfortunately, the AFL uniformly supported the Monroe Doctrine, typically under the guise of fighting communism— but in actual fact to promote U.S. business interests. Shortsightedly, Gompers believed that union members in the United States would benefit because U.S. corporations would be more profitable and could afford to pay higher wages. Initially, the CIO was often in opposition to government foreign policy, but this changed dramatically during the early Cold War, and by the time of the merger, the two organizations were pretty much in synch in terms of international affairs.

Under the auspices of the State Department, the CIA, and business leaders such as the Rockefellers, organized labor in the United States became part of several ostensible labor organizations in Latin America, such as the Inter-American Regional Organization of Workers (ORIT) formed in 1951. But these proved inadequate to the task of promoting pro-American unions abroad, especially after the Cuban revolution threatened to unleash radical nationalism throughout the region. So in 1961 the American Institute for Free Labor Development (AIFLD) was established to promote "free" trade unionism (freed of communist influence) in Latin America. The AIFLD is a part of the AFL-CIO but receives almost all of its funds from the U.S. State Department. It has closely collaborated with American business interests, including some of the most notorious exploiters of Latin American resources, workers, and peasants, as well as the CIA and corrupt local governments. Its budgets are closely guarded secrets, and its books have never been independently audited. Needless to say, it is a rare union member who knows anything about it.

The record of AIFLD has been a disaster for the world's labor movements. It helped to plan the military coup against the democratic government of Brazil in 1964. It supported the coup which overthrew the Allende government in Chile. It seldom challenged ruthless military governments, even those which had AIFLD operatives killed. Among the governments with which it has had cordial relationships are those of Guatemala, where more than one hundred thousand peasants and workers were murdered after the coup of 1954, a coup organized by the United States and supported by the AFL;[39] El Salvador, which waged a brutal war against peasants and workers throughout the 1980s;[40] and Nicaragua under the authoritarian Somozas. After Somoza was overthrown by the Sandinista revolution in 1979, AIFLD began to foment strikes and sabotage against the new government.[41] This made Nicaragua the only country in Central American in which the AIFLD urged actions which unions normally take. In other countries with governments more to Washington's liking, AIFLD concentrated on programs for small farmers, education, collaboration with employers, and the disruption and defeat of more militant unions. AIFLD leaders and most AFL-CIO leaders supported the criminal *contra* war against the Sandinista government and very probably gave direct financial aid to the *contras*. All of these damaged progressive trade unionism in countries among the poorest in the world, where strong, aggressive unions and political organizations are most needed. In the long run they undermined the cause of U.S. workers, as well, by depressing competitive wage rates, making plant relocation profitable in coming decades.

THE TIME IS RIPE

Unlike workers in most of the rest of the world, labor in the United States has been unable to form its own political parties. Unions have instead worked within the two-party structure, acting as a pressure group, mainly within the Democratic Party. This "pragmatic" politics has never worked especially well to promote the interests of the working class, and events over the past three decades indicate that if labor continues to pursue a "pragmatic" strategy, it will court real disaster. The long postwar boom in the U.S. economy ended in the early 1970s. In response, employers began a massive restructuring of their workplaces. Plants were closed or moved overseas in search of cheap labor. Mergers and buyouts created huge conglomerates of capital prepared to move money around the globe irrespective of domestic consequences. Work arrangements were revolutionized to minimize the employers' dependence on any particular group of workers and to sharply intensify work effort. The attack upon unions escalated, with employers routinely refusing to bargain in good faith and committing numerous illegal acts whenever their workers tried to unionize.

Employers began to lobby relentlessly against any reforms of the labor laws. At the same time, they pushed for labor laws more attuned to their new strategies (for example, the abolition of the NLRA's prohibition of company unions, so that the new "teams" could not be legally challenged); for elimination of restrictions on international movement of capital (as in NAFTA and similar trade agreements); for the drastic curtailment of environmental, health, and safety regulations and anti-trust provisions; and for the shredding of the social safety net, including slashes to public assistance, medical care, unemployment compensation, and social security. Employers were nonpartisan in their efforts, enlisting the support of sympathetic Republicans and Democrats alike.

"Labor law reform is supported by millions . . . unfortunately that's people, not dollars."   [Carol/Simpson]

A sophisticated propaganda campaign was engineered to win public support for their agenda. Americans were told that the world had become increasingly competitive and that the United States could not survive this competition unless it did what business wanted. With market forces "inevitably" changing the world economy, American workers were warned to get in tune with what the markets dictated or sink into an economic swamp of low growth and falling living standards. Business funded a host of think tanks and propagandists to promote its agenda.

Since the mid-1970s, politicians of both parties have bent over backwards to implement what amounts to a full-scale assault on working people. By any measure, working class living standards began to plummet, shored up only by borrowing and excessive workdays. The rich have gotten richer, while workers have gotten progressively poorer. What should the labor movement do in the face of all of this? Until the election of new leadership in the AFL-CIO in 1995, organized labor did very little to combat capital's war on the working class. Fighting back was left to various grassroots groups, including some within the ranks of labor, but their valiant efforts were too localized and piecemeal to reverse labor's decline. The new leadership claims that it wants to rebuild the labor movement. What are its chances?

Let us make a logical argument. First, the Republican and the Democratic parties are obviously allied with and subservient to the most powerful employers in the nation. The Republicans may seem to be more ruthless and transparent in their willingness to obey the dictates of capital, but the Democrats, in practice, are no different. In fact, the Democrats are often more dangerous to workers, because they have a reputation for being the friends of labor. Democrats usually campaign on a worker-friendly program, but this is largely hype. Once in office, they do the bidding of employers just as surely as the Republicans. And since they are perceived to be more liberal than they are, they are able to get away with more vicious attacks on workers than the Republicans. They gut welfare and support NAFTA while giving lip service to liberal social causes like a clean environment and abortion rights. In a pinch, they say that they are helpless to do anything of benefit to workers because of the overwhelming power of the Republicans. But look at who funds both parties and who serves in the administrations of both parties—Wall Street financiers, corporate lawyers, corporate executives, and other assorted wealthy individuals, almost without exception.

Second, labor's natural constituency is comprised of those hurt by the policies of both political parties. A labor movement is made up of nonsupervisory workers, together with the unemployed and the poor who are not in the labor force. A labor movement must ally itself with groups that support the interests of these people, including community, religious, environmental, and civil rights organizations, both here and abroad. In other words, a labor movement is, by definition, a movement of those opposed to employers. Therefore, labor's politics should be a politics of opposition to capital and support of workers and their allies. The Democratic Party has long since abandoned any allegiance to working people (indeed, its alliance with labor during the Great Depression must be considered an exceptional result of its own self-interest and the open revolt of workers). It is now a party of capital every bit as much as the Republican Party. If organized labor ties its star to the Democratic Party, it is tying itself to its class enemy.

Third, if labor continues to conduct its politics within the Democratic Party, it cannot hope to be fully accepted by its natural constituency, because it will not be able to fully champion the causes of that constituency. When Democratic politicians must promote the interests of employers, as a consequence of who they are and who pays their bills, labor will be forced to knuckle under or risk its own status in the party. Thus union officials will not offend the Democrats by rejecting their open ravaging of the social safety net. Thus unions will give support to an anti-labor foreign policy—for example, the war in Vietnam—which usually pits the United States against working people worldwide. Thus unions will support any Democratic candidate for president or other high office, irrespective of that candidate's labor record. Labor officials will argue that the Democrats are the lesser evil or that they do not want to risk Democratic support for certain labor objectives. But today the Democratic Party's main interests are not those of working people, and when push comes to shove, Democrats will show up in capital's corner. In such a circumstance, labor may win an occasional battle, as when Clinton finally supported an increase in the minimum wage, but it will lose the war.

Labor's need is to develop a politics of its own, an independent politics, one to which it holds no matter what policies are promoted by the two parties of capital. If it fails to do so, it may as well give up hope of revitalizing its cause.

CHAPTER SIX

UNIONS, RACISM, AND SEXISM

The U.S. working class has always been a diverse mix, in part because of the continuous transformation of the labor process. As capitalism develops, new skills are created and old ones destroyed, with each change bringing forth new diversity in the labor force.[1] At the beginning of capitalist production, employers were forced to rely upon skilled workers, because work in pre-capitalist society was not yet subdivided and deskilled. Once capitalists began to employ a detailed division of labor, a split was created between skilled and unskilled workers. Skilled workers were the first to form labor unions, because they could see that the employer needed them and would pay them more if they stuck together. These unions often did not see a need to organize their unskilled brothers and sisters; in fact, it was not uncommon for them to look down upon the unskilled. Some occupations require various types of specialized formal training, and this has often created categories of *professional* employees. Professionals, too, sometimes tend to look with disdain upon other types of workers. Needless to say, employers find it in their interest to exacerbate feelings of difference that reduce the likelihood of groups joining together against them. Thus, my own employer argued during our union drive that unions were fine for coal miners and steel workers but not for professors. Sometimes skilled workers embrace this argument on their own: during the 1930s, for example, the craft workers in the AFL butchers' union showed no interest in organizing their less skilled counterparts in the stockyards.[2]

In some unions, leadership remains exclusively white and male. Here, AFL-CIO President John Sweeney poses with Ironworkers union officials at the federation convention, 1997. [Jim West]

The establishment of a privileged tier of workers is only one of many divisions in the working class, some of which predate capitalism. Work has always been done by both men and women, but gender differences take on specific characteristics in capitalist economies. Throughout most of our history, for example, women have been concentrated in certain types of work, often taking the form of extensions of the unpaid household labor which traditionally they have been expected to perform. Domestic work, primary school teaching, secretarial work, and nursing are occupations that have been and still are overwhelmingly female.[3] The skilled trades, such as carpentry, plumbing, and construction labor of all types, have been reserved for men. Men have resisted, sometimes with violence, the entry of women into "male" jobs. Naturally, this impedes the development of common collective actions by men and women.

Religion, ethnicity, race, and sexual orientation have also divided workers at one time or another in our history. Irish immigrants suffered terribly at the hands of native workers and were confined to the worst jobs for many years. Employment ads appeared in newspapers which stated, "Irish need not apply."

Similar discrimination has been the lot of nearly every non-Anglo-Saxon group which came to the United States, as well as some religious communities, especially Jews.[4] Gay and lesbian workers have suffered brutal discrimination and, unlike the other groups discussed in this chapter, still do not enjoy protection under our civil rights laws. However, in the United States the sharpest divide has been racial. The great majority of African Americans spent their first 250 years here as slaves, and the racism which that inhumane system spawned is still with us.[5] After the Civil War, black workers were systematically excluded from skilled labor and from most unskilled industrial jobs as well. It was not until the 1920s that appreciable numbers of black workers gained employment in our mass production industries, and it was not until the 1960s that they were able to make inroads into skilled and professional work. It has not been uncommon for employers to play the "race card" for all it is worth to keep employees disorganized and weak, although white workers often needed no encouragement to act out of racism. Employers have sometimes recruited black workers as strikebreakers, inflaming racial tensions and bringing down the wrath of white strikers upon blacks.[6] Some black workers used as strike-breakers in the meatpacking plants in the early 1920s were kept on by the companies for the specific purpose of fomenting antagonisms within the workforce.

While diversity has always characterized the U.S. workforce, the nature of the diversity has undergone significant changes between the early years of capitalist industrialization and the present. In 1890, only 17 percent of the labor force was female, and of all women in the labor force, just 13 percent were married. Women in the labor force were more likely to be from the poorer classes; white married women were unlikely to be working for wages unless their families were very poor. The occupations open to women were limited. Of the 5.3 million women in the labor force in 1900, nearly 30 percent worked as servants in private households. For certain women, especially blacks, private household labor was all that was available. At the turn of the century, most African Americans still worked in agriculture, although few owned farms. Still, African Americans also worked for wages in industries outside of agriculture, as did immigrants from Mexico, Japan, China, and the Philippines, in mining, laundries, restaurants, railroad construction, and the garment industry.[7]

TABLE 3

UNION MEMBERS BY SEX AND RACE, 1995[12]

	Group Members	All Union Members	Union Density
Total	16,359,600	100%	14.9%
Men	9,929,300	60.7%	17.2%
Women	6,430,300	39.3%	12.3%
White	13,149,500	80.4%	14.2%
Black	2,519,100	15.4%	19.9%
Other	691,100	4.2%	14.9%
(Hispanic)	(1,356,900)	(8.3%)	(13.1%)

Note: Hispanics may be white or black or other in the racial breakdown, so they are listed separately.

Three trends stand out since the Second World War, which had a tremendous impact on the composition of the labor force, opening up new sectors to women and people of color. First, the labor force participation of women has risen rapidly. In 1995, nearly 60 percent of women over twenty years of age were in the labor force; women will very soon comprise half of the entire labor force. Furthermore, the labor force participation of married women with children has been increasing more rapidly than that of women as a whole.[8] The notion that married women should not work for wages was never completely applicable to the poorest families; now it has been discarded by nearly all families. Second, there has been a massive shift of minority workers out of agriculture and personal services into other types of work.[9] This is not to say that African Americans, for example, are represented proportionally in all occupations. Quite the contrary, they are still more likely to be in the worst paying, most difficult, and dirtiest jobs. Within a given workplace, moreover, jobs are still highly segregated, so that whites and nonwhites do not usually work together. Yet black workers make up significant proportions in many manufacturing industries and in a range of services. Minority workers have made significant inroads into the public sector, largely as a result of the civil rights movement and decades of litigation.[10] Third, new entrants into our labor force are increasingly likely to be black, Hispanic, and Asian. Today nonwhites make up about one-quarter of the entire labor force.[11]

In Table 3, we see that total union membership in the United States in 1995 was approximately 16,359,600. The third column shows the percentage of total union membership made up by a particular group. We see that 15.4 percent of all union members are African-American, and, given that this group comprises only about 11 percent of the labor force, it is overrepresented among union members. Women, on the other hand, make up 39.3 percent of all union members, but because they comprise a larger fraction of the labor force, they are underrepresented in unions. The final column shows the fraction of employed workers from particular groups which belongs to unions, or the *union density*. In the United States, only 14.9 percent of all employees are union members, one of the lowest union densities in all of the advanced capitalist nations. However, note that the union density for blacks is significantly higher than for whites. This means that black workers are more likely than white workers to be union members. Women, however, have a lower density than do men.

Union membership, like the labor force itself, is diverse, and is becoming more so. The share of minority workers and women in total union membership is growing. Yet, union densities for all groups have been falling. If unions are to grow, if they are to meet the challenge of a multiracial and gendered economy, they must organize more women and more people of color.[13] (Not that white male workers can be neglected; their union densities are extremely low and falling, but they will continue to account for a sizable share of the labor force for many years to come.)

UNIONS, RACISM, AND JUSTICE

Racism has cast a long shadow in the United States, from the slaughter of Native Americans and the theft of their lands to the enslavement of Africans and the brutal treatment of their descendants to the routine cruelties meted out to Hispanics, Asians, and other people of color. White workers have hardly been immune to this racism, nor have the unions which U.S. workers have formed.[14] Under slavery, African Americans did all kinds of tasks, from backbreaking labor in the fields to highly skilled crafts. After the Civil War, they hoped to be able to pursue whatever work they were capable of doing, but this was not to be. White workers, employers, and public officials drove them out of the skilled trades and denied them work in many unskilled occupations as well. The craft unions which formed the AFL systematically barred black workers; most of the early craft unions and all of the railroad brotherhoods had race restrictions in their constitutions, and some of these remained in effect into the 1960s. Even left-wing labor organizations sometimes excluded African Americans, including Eugene V. Debs's American Railway Union, although this was done against Debs's wishes. Chinese workers were the victims of special wrath; remarkably, even some unions formed by black workers excluded them from membership. Samuel Gompers wrote a pamphlet in which he condemned Chinese immigrants for bringing "nothing but filth, vice, and disease." Gompers must not have remembered the railroads and the many Chinese laborers who worked to death building them for employers who were responsible for the "filth, vice, and disease." A few early labor organizations were notable for their racial egalitarianism, for example, the Knights of Labor and the IWW, but these were a distinct minority. And occasionally workers of different races joined in struggle against employers. In the 1890s, for example, black and white dockworkers at the port of New Orleans came together in a general strike. Events of this type, however, were anomalies.[15]

As industrialization sped up during the first decades of this century, the composition of the labor force began to change, at least in major industries. Change came first to the South, where in 1900, 90 percent of all African-Americans still lived. African Americans became more numerous in industries such as coal and ore mining, iron and steel production, dockworking, railroads, tobacco and food processing, textiles, and lumbering. When economic and political forces began to drive blacks out of Southern agriculture, they began a long period of migration north, where they performed largely unskilled labor in the automobile factories, packinghouses, rubber plants, and other mass production workplaces which would be the centers of the union upsurge of the 1930s. Similar trajectories were followed by other minorities, albeit with different timing and sometimes in different industries.[16] Thus, at the time when workers began to organize industrial unions, minority workers sometimes comprised significant fractions of the workforce and occupied strategic jobs. Successful unionization, therefore, required multiracial organizations.

The CIO unions and leadership differed sharply from the traditionally racist AFL, and this was especially the case when the new unions were led by socialists and communists.[17] Some scholars have argued that the CIO's attitude toward race was strictly pragmatic; it was not possible to build strong unions in mass-production industries (unlike the crafts) unless minority workers, usually African-American, supported the unions. However, this view overlooks the interracial egalitarianism of many union leaders, at both local and national levels, which reflected a deeply held worldview. For example, the UMW had a long history of organizing black miners, insisting upon their equal treatment by the companies, and it did this in the South, where the risks were extremely high.[18] The egalitarianism of the UMW changed the attitudes of many white miners, making them willing to defend their black brothers and to socialize with them at union functions. What can be said about the UMW can also be said about many other unions during the 1930s and 1940s. The anti-racism of the early CIO was obvious enough to lead the great black scholar and activist, W. E. B. Du Bois, to say this:

> Probably the greatest and most effective effort toward interracial understanding among the working masses has come about through the trade unions. . . . As a result [of the organization of the CIO in 1935], numbers of men like those in the steel and automotive industries have been thrown together, black and white, as fellow workers striving for the same objects. There has been on this account an astonishing spread of interracial tolerance and understanding. Probably no movement in the last 30 years has been so successful in softening race prejudice among the masses.[19]

Of course, the extent to which unions attacked racism and continued to extend the rights of minority workers varied greatly from union to union. Some unions had few minority workers but aggressively fought for them and for civil rights in the larger society: the Fur and Leather Workers Union, the Farm Equipment Workers, and the National Maritime Union. Some, like the Food, Tobacco, and Agricultural Workers, the Mine, Mill, and Smelter Workers Union, and the United Packinghouse Workers Union, with substantial or majority black memberships, not only built their unions upon a foundation of anti-racism but continued to deepen their members' commitment to this throughout their existence. And these unions achieved black-white solidarity not just in the cities of the North but in the South as well, disproving the all but universal belief that white workers in the South would never accept blacks as equals. It is true that there were some left-wing unions which did not always live up to their anti-racist ideology.[20] But it can be said with some certainty that the unions with strong left-wing leadership set the standard by which unions could be (and, for the most part, can still be) judged in terms of racial equality.

Against these examples of racial solidarity can be set the actions of other CIO unions— and, of course, nearly all of the AFL unions and the railroad brotherhoods. The United Steelworkers abandoned the theme of racial unity soon after the industry was organized. Under the leadership of Philip Murray, the union quickly purged the radicals who helped organize the workers and established a top-down method of leadership with little respect for rank-and-file initiative. Not surprisingly, the union negotiated agreements which, through the rule of departmental seniority, excluded black workers from the better jobs, condemning them to lifetimes in the hottest, dirtiest, and most dangerous departments. Under departmental seniority, a black worker who transferred out of a low-paying and dirty department like the coke plant and into a better department would have zero seniority in the new department. If there was a layoff in the new department, he would be the first worker let go, despite the fact that he might have had more plant seniority than every white worker in the department.[21] Similar conditions prevailed in the more liberal United Auto Workers, where the skilled jobs in the plants were reserved strictly for white workers. Both of these unions participated fully in the anticommunist witch-hunts at the start of the Cold War, ridding themselves of many leaders committed to racial equality. This period also coincided with the CIO's abandonment of its "Operation Dixie" drive to organize the South, in which unions like the United Packinghouse Workers of America and the left-led unions purged from the CIO had shown that it was possible, even in the face of legally enforced Jim Crow segregation, to form interracial unions and begin the difficult task of breaking down white worker racism.

THE UNITED PACKINGHOUSE WORKERS[22]

Working in a packinghouse, preparing animals for our supermarkets, is, by all accounts, a little like laboring in hell. Imagine extremes of hot and cold, vile smells, blood all over the place, sharp knives, slippery floors, and a killing pace, and you might begin to get the idea. Just the names of the jobs is chilling: stockhandlers, knockers, shacklers, stickers, beheaders, hide removers, skinners, leg-breakers, foot-skinners, backers, rumpers, hide-droppers, butchers, gut-snatchers, gutters, splitters, and luggers. And the key workers are those on the "killing floor." No wonder black workers made early inroads in the packing houses; white workers went elsewhere if they had the chance. By the 1930s, African-Americans made up an important share of the workers in the Chicago stockyards and some other areas. When the union bug bit stockyard workers, these black workers could not be ignored, especially since they often worked the killing floors, the first stage of work in the slaughtering of animals and the operation upon which the rest depended.

Out of these industrial charnel houses in Chicago, Kansas City, Sioux City, and Austin, Minnesota, there arose a remarkable union: the United Packinghouse Workers of America (UPWA), a radical, rank-and-file controlled union in which black and white workers came together, not just to better their working conditions and wage rates—which they did—but also to fight for civil rights in the factories and their communities. Led by radicals of various stripes (Wobblies, socialists, and communists), packinghouse workers moved from the lowest rung of industrial workers to among the highest. At every level of the union, black workers were leaders, and they helped to build a union in the 1940s and 1950s which was one of the most interracial organizations in the nation. Unlike many other CIO unions, the UPWA made racial issues a focus of their union efforts, and it never purged its radical leaders. Furthermore, the union maintained local control over the national union and never gave up the local unions' right to strike; nor did it shy away from actions of dubious legality when struggling for control over the pace of work.

Concretely, the UPWA achieved the following contractual provisions which were instrumental in winning equality for black workers: (1) equal pay for equal work; (2) an end to lower wages for Southern workers, many of whom were black; (3) open access to the highest paying jobs; (4) the continuation of seniority during layoffs, so that black men and women who entered meatpacking during the Second World War could get their jobs back when employment levels regained their wartime highs; and (5) an anti-discrimination clause which not only prohibited discrimination against employees but also against "applicants," so that the union could attack discrimination in hiring. In connection with this last provision, writes historian Roger Horowitz,

> In 1950 the Swift union arranged for both black and white women to apply for jobs and carefully monitored the employment office to determine the company's response to the applicants. While white women were courteously ushered into a back room, interviewed, and then hired, company officials brusquely turned black women away with the excuse that there were no openings. The local filed a grievance against Swift and won a landmark ruling requiring the company to hire the black women with back pay from the date they had initially applied. The international union widely publicized the Chicago victory and pressed other local unions to follow a similar strategy.[23]

Largely because the rest of the labor movement had refused to follow the lead of the UPWA, the union was not able to resist the radical restructuring of the industry in the 1960s, 1970s, and 1980s. Plants in the union strongholds were closed and moved to nonunion rural areas, a move made possible in part by technological changes in both the packing of meat and its distribution. The union simply did not have the resources to organize the new plants, and the rest of labor did not see fit to help. Today, the gains won by the UPWA have been largely reversed, and the Latino, Asian, and poor white workers who prepare our meat work under conditions not unlike those which prevailed before the UPWA waged its heroic struggles.

BLACK AND LATINO UNIONISM

Some unions have had overwhelmingly minority memberships, and in these unions the connections between issues of race and class were always clear. Two examples are the Brotherhood of Sleeping Car Porters and the United Farm Workers.[24] The Brotherhood of Sleeping Car Porters was founded in 1925 by black socialist A. Philip Randolph. The Pullman Company (the one which had helped to destroy Debs's American Railway Union in the 1890s) employed some 15,000 black porters on its railroad sleeping cars, making it the largest employer of black workers in the country. For white Americans, the subservience which porters were obliged to show passengers made this fitting work for African Americans. The average porter worked four hundred hours a month and traveled eleven thousand miles. Nevertheless, given the job segregation which black workers faced, this was good employment and attracted many talented and well-educated workers. Porters flocked to the union banner despite their cool reception from the AFL, which refused to charter a national union of porters. When the union was not able to force the Pullman company to recognize the union and bargain a contract, many porters quit the union in disgust. But the union revived itself during the Great Depression, winning membership in the AFL in 1936, a year after a federal mediation board had certified it as the official representative of the porters. In 1937 it finally won an agreement with Pullman, with significant benefits for the workers.

At the same time, Randolph became a major spokesman for African-American workers, and, in alliance with other black groups, including some with Communist ties, formed the National Negro Congress. Among many other civil rights activities, the congress urged the CIO to organize black working people. Within the AFL, Randolph worked tirelessly to get the organization to end its racism, but his efforts had only moderate success. In 1941, he called for a march on Washington to pressure the government to end discrimination in the plants producing goods for the war. In response, President Roosevelt issued Executive Order 8802, which prohibited such discrimination and established the Fair Employment Practices Committee; Randolph declared victory and called off the march. Again, these legal gains had mixed results and did not end segregation, but they showed that black unionists were a force to be reckoned with by employers, the government, and organized labor.

The United Farm Workers (UFW) was founded in the early 1960s out of a merger of unions formed by Filipino and Chicano workers in the Southwest. The leader of the UFW was Cesar Chavez, who had been a farm worker since his parents had lost their small farm in Arizona during the Great Depression. Chavez built the union into a formidable social movement, utilizing nationwide consumer boycotts and strikes, and attracting hundreds of idealistic young people as volunteers to make these direct actions work. During the

1960s, Mexican-Americans had begun to demand a place at the American table and to forge a civil rights movement. Chavez was an extraordinary, charismatic leader, adept at using a combination of civil rights rhetoric and religious symbolism to electrify migrant farm workers. His famous grape boycott helped to bring some of California's growers and wineries to the bargaining table to win for farm workers more of the fruits of their backbreaking labors. As the UFW grew into a social movement, it was able to secure passage of state legislation guaranteeing farm workers the rights which most private sector workers had enjoyed since passage of the NLRA. (Agricultural workers are not covered by the federal labor laws.) The California Agricultural Labor Relations Act of 1970 even went beyond the NLRA in providing monetary penalties against employers refusing to bargain. After 1970, the UFW won hundreds of union representation elections and secured hundreds of collective bargaining agreements.

The growers never accepted this union of their social "inferiors," and they waged ceaseless war against it. Many of the victories of the early years were undone in the late 1970s and the 1980s. The growers got the Teamsters union to challenge the UFW and began to sign "sweetheart" contracts with the then-corrupt Teamsters. Then they used their enormous political power to undermine the collective bargaining law. Beset by these external forces and racked by internal tensions which led to the firing and resignation of most of the union's best organizers and staff, the union had sunk into impotence by the time of Chavez's death in 1993. However, under the leadership of Chavez's son-in-law, Arturo Rodriquez, the union has begun a comeback. It has mounted a campaign, with strong support from the new AFL-CIO leadership, to organize workers for California's 270 strawberry growers.[25] Combining job actions, boycotts, and community organizing, the union hopes to regain its lost glory and help the thousands of farm laborers who are no better off today than they were when John Steinbeck published *The Grapes of Wrath* in 1939.

UFW headquarters is in a former sanitarium in Keene, California, which is located in the Tehachapi Mountains, about thirty miles east of Bakersfield. It is called "La Paz." I lived there during the winter and spring of 1977 when I served as the union's research director. I was one of the scores of union volunteers who lived there more or less communally, serving the union. It was one of the most memorable experiences of my life. I will never forget my first union meeting in a small town down the mountain, not far from the former location of the government camp made famous in *The Grapes of Wrath.* Hundreds of men and women, most speaking little English and not one of them yet under contract, met, discussed their union and problems with the growers, and sang songs. Dirt poor and excluded from the mainstream of American life, they had banded together in this wonderful union, ready to risk their lives for the cause. I was overwhelmed by their friendliness and gratitude that I had come to work for them. Scenes like this were repeated many times during my stay in California, at the bargaining table with farm workers, at court hearings, at demonstrations, in door-to-door electoral campaigning—Mexicans, Chicanos, Filipinos, Palestinians, finding power in the simple idea of a union, of a movement greater than themselves.

UNIONS AND WOMEN

Our nation's first industrial workers were the rural New England women recruited to work in the textile mills. Ever since, women have been wage laborers. Today, women's participation in the labor force is rapidly approaching that of men. The experiences of women with labor unions are to some degree akin to the experiences of racial minorities. That is, women workers have faced deep discrimination within the labor movement, but there have been examples of successful unionization, as well as solidarity between male and female workers.[26]

There are, however, at least three significant differences between the labor union experiences of women and those of minority workers. First, gender segregation in wage labor has often been even more profound than racial segregation between workers of the same sex. Women have been concentrated in certain occupations in which there have sometimes been literally no male co-workers. This meant that the male-dominated AFL and CIO usually saw no need to make serious efforts to organize women. There were exceptions, such as female textile and garment workers, who by the force of their own self-organization compelled organized labor to take notice. Yet even in cases of successful unionization, unions in which women were a significant proportion of the members, or even most of the members, have usually been run by men.

TABLE 4

FEMALE MEMBERSHIP AND LEADERSHIP IN CERTAIN UNIONS, 1994[27]

Union	Women as Proportion of Members	Women Officers and Board Members	Women as Proportion of Officers and Board Members
NEA	65-70%	4	44%
Teamsters	20-30%	1	4%
UFCW	51%	3	8%
AFSCME	52%	5	16%
SEIU	50%	13	24%
AFT	70%	13	32%
CWA	51%	3	21%
IBEW	30%	0	0%
ACTWU*	61%	4	19%
ILGWU*	85%	4	21%
HERE	48% (1990)	2 (1994)	9.1% (1994)

These two unions have merged to form UNITE. As of 1996, the union had nine women officers and board members, 29 percent of the total.

The American Federation of Teachers (AFT) is a case in point. Most public school teachers are women, but the top leadership of the union has until very recently been male.

Second, even in unions which were very progressive on the race question, women have been second-class citizens. In the meatpacking industry, women were concentrated in certain jobs, most of which paid less than those performed by men. The United Packinghouse Workers, although one of the labor movement's most egalitarian unions, did not fight for an abolition of male-female job distinctions. The UPWA did demand and get equal pay for equal work; that is, if a woman did a job ordinarily done by a man, she got the same pay. The trouble was that she almost never did get such jobs. To its great credit, the UPWA forced the packinghouses to honor the seniority that female workers accumulated during the Second World War. It did not discourage women from taking leadership roles, especially within the locals, and it held special meetings

(Gary Huck)

and conferences dedicated to issues important to women workers. But it was not until some women filed suits against both the employers and the union under the 1964 Civil Rights Act that the segregated job classification system was eliminated. Unfortunately, the corporate destruction of the unionized sector of the meatpacking industry meant that not many women got to enjoy the fruits of their efforts.[28]

Third (and intimately tied to the first two distinctions), unlike male workers of all races and ethnic backgrounds, women have borne and still bear the primary responsibility for raising children and holding families together. An ideological underpinning of the early labor movement, and one which still has a hold on many men, was that it was the duty of a man to support his family financially and the duty of a woman to keep the home fires burning. The unions pressed employers to pay a "family wage," one large enough for the husband to support the family without the wife working for wages. This ideology generated resentment on the part of male workers who thought that women workers were taking jobs that would otherwise go to male breadwinners, thereby undermining the family. In addition, it helped to foster the belief that there must be something wrong with a woman who worked: a woman "outside the home" was suspected of being morally "loose" or just not "good enough" to land a man. Of course, the realities of working-class life dictated that women work for wages, but the ideology militated against taking their work seriously. After the Second World War, for example, most men and even many women saw it as the duty of women to leave the labor force and give the jobs back to the returning male ex-soldiers who were their legitimate "owners."

Throughout the great postwar economic expansion, women continued to increase their presence in the labor market and in union workplaces. But just as the labor movement was not in the frontlines of the black and Latino civil rights struggles, so too was it dragged, often kicking and screaming, into the fight for gender equality. The collapse of working-class standards of living which began in the early 1970s and coincided with a rapid decline in union membership has forced families to send more members into the workforce. Women's hours of wage work have risen dramatically as a consequence, and unions have been forced to address women's concerns, both to accommodate increasingly stressed female union members, and to rebuild the labor movement to reflect the influx of women into the labor force.[29] Naturally, this is not to say that unions have never promoted the interests of women, since this is not the case.[30] The AFL-CIO has long been on record as strongly supportive of public policies, such as the Equal Rights Amendment, which benefit women. However, now there is a move to better match the rhetoric of the past with concrete actions.

WOMEN IN STRUGGLE

Despite the barriers placed in front of them, working women have been the stuff of labor legend. One of the most famous women unionists was Mary "Mother" Jones, who worked to organize coal miners until she was quite advanced in years. When the miners went out on strike, she led brigades of women and children, marching and banging pots and pans, in the coal towns of Pennsylvania to support the men.[31] Here are a few other examples given to me by labor historian and educator Priscilla Murolo:

• After the Civil War, African-American women were often forced, out of necessity, to seek wage labor. The only jobs available to them were in domestic service, although the hatred of slavery made them unwilling, unless absolutely necessary, to live in the homes of former masters. They therefore preferred a job such as washerwoman, in which they could do the work in their own homes and return the cleaned clothes to the employer, thereby maintaining some autonomy and the ability to care for their families. Employers hated this and tried repeatedly to force the washerwomen back into a slave-like servility. In response to employer antagonism, Atlanta's washerwomen conducted a massive strike in the summer of 1891, building large-scale community support despite threats of taxation from public officials, arrests, and violence. This strike encouraged other black workers to take collective actions against the multiple repressions which they faced.[32]

• In 1909, more than twenty thousand female garment workers in some five hundred New York City shops struck against the deplorable conditions in which they labored and lived. They worked eleven to fourteen hours per day in hot (or cold), dangerous, cramped sweatshops, without decent drinking water, under the direction of brutal foremen. At home, conditions were similar: large families crowded into dirty and dangerous tenements. When several women workers at the Triangle Shirtwaist Company admitted that they were members of the new International Ladies' Garment Workers' Union (ILGWU), their employer told them that no more work was available for them. They picketed the shop and were beaten by company-hired thugs and arrested by the police. It looked like they were defeated, but the Women's Trade Union League, established in 1903 by workers and liberal sympathizers to help women workers, entered the dispute. The League publicized the horrible working conditions and helped build solidarity to the point that the garment workers organized a general strike. Over the next few months, thousands of strikers were beaten and arrested, but in the end, with help from workers around the country, they prevailed and made the ILGWU into a powerful union.[33]

• In Lawrence, Massachusetts, in 1912, textile employers responded to a state law restricting the hours of work for women and children by cutting their workers' pay. Years of abuse, which resulted in extremely high rates of infant mortality, childhood diseases, rampant child labor, and crippling and disease-causing work conditions, pushed the women laborers to respond with a spontaneous strike at the American Woolen Company. The strike spread throughout the city, and was soon aided by the IWW, which sent its best organizers to Lawrence, including the famous firebrand Elizabeth Gurley Flynn. Met with fierce repression, including the police beating of pregnant women, the strikers responded with mass picketing: thousands of workers circled the factory, arm in arm, around the clock. Faced with starvation, strikers sent their children to New York and other towns and cities to stay with sympathizers, a move which was met with police clubbings at the train station. Finally, the U.S. Congress investigated the strike and held hearings at which mill children gave moving testimony. The strength and endurance of the strikers, along with the bad publicity generated by police and corporate brutality, forced the companies to settle the strike. Lawrence became known as the "Bread and Roses" strike, because the strikers fought not just for more pay but for a chance to enjoy some of life's pleasures. "Yes, it is bread we fight for," they sang, "But we fight for roses too."[34]

• In the late 1930s, packing and canning workers, most of them Chicanas and Mexicanas, formed a remarkable union: the United Cannery, Agricultural, Packing, and Allied Workers of America (UCAPAWA).[35] Building upon the close social relationships which existed in their communities and in their workplaces, these women succeeded in challenging the power of California's growers and packers, winning strong collective bargaining agreements which not only protected them as workers but as women as well. The national union was developed from the ground up (similar to the UPWA) and was a model of democracy, with women participating at every level of the union's governance. Over the next decade, the union organized packers and canners, migrant farm workers, pecan shellers, and southern tobacco workers. Led by a band of radicals, including its president Donald Henderson, UCAPAWA faced down vigilantes, sheriffs, and police to organize some of society's most exploited workers. Membership grew remarkably under the boom conditions of the Second World War, and the union took advantage of labor shortages to greatly improve the wages and conditions of the workers. The union also operated labor schools and held numerous social events to unify and educate the members. Eventually it changed its name to the Food, Tobacco, Agricultural, and Allied Workers of America (FTA) to reflect its changing membership, but its policies remained steadfastly militant and inclusive.

Sadly, this wonderful union was destroyed after the war by a combination of redbaiting, legal persecution, and raiding by the Teamsters. But its legacy lives on. Between 1985 and 1987, hundreds of workers, mostly Chicanas, struck for eighteen months and defeated Watsonville Cannery and at the same time returned their

Teamster-led union back to the strategies and tactics of their old union, UCAPAWA.[36]

• In 1984 and 1985, female clerical workers brought mighty Yale University to a halt when it refused to negotiate with their union. The union was formed through patient grassroots organizing which focused directly on the lower pay of women (and especially women of color) who did work directly comparable, although not the same, to the work male workers did in the university. The Ivy League school responded by hiring well-paid union busters to defeat the union organizing drive and to stall the bargaining after the union's election victory. The women fought back by organizing students, teachers, the male union of custodians and maintenance employees, and townspeople in support of their efforts to win decent wages from one of the richest schools in the world and New Haven's biggest employer. Picketing, street demonstrations and blockades, and innovative strike tactics (the women returned to work at one point in the bargaining to recoup lost wages) conquered Yale's administrators and built a formidable union.[37]

INTERSECTION OF RACE AND GENDER

Historically women of color have had higher labor force participation rates than those of white women, and many of the new entrants into the labor force today are also women of color, often newly-arrived immigrants from Asia and Latin America. Some unions are making special efforts to organize women of color.[38]

Take the garment industry. Just as at the beginning of this century, when the unions of garment workers were formed, most garment workers today are immigrant women, although most now are immigrant women of color. As in the earlier period, most of the women work for low wages under deplorable conditions. Large clothing companies like Levi's and The Gap, as well as purveyors of designer clothing, use contractors to get the actual work done. The contractors, in turn, subcontract the work to shops, of which there are many thousands. In small shops in cities like Los Angeles and New York, women make dresses, pants, and jeans, often taking work home with them. Their employers flagrantly violate all of the labor laws, paying them below minimum wage (often not paying them at all), denying them overtime wages, and ignoring health and safety laws and codes.[39] So it was nothing out of the ordinary when twelve Asian women from a Bay Area sweatshop came to the Asian Immigrant Women Advocates (AIWA) to complain that their boss had not paid them. AIWA is a community organization formed in 1983 to address the myriad problems faced by Asian immigrant women. The twelve women, acting with the AIWA, developed a campaign to get back their lost wages.

Their immediate employer had declared bankruptcy, a common tactic among subcontractors, who then turn around and open another shop under a new name. However, this employer supplied clothing for a number of well-known designers, including fashion designer Jessica McClintock. The women and the AIWA decided to go after McClintock, arguing that the manufacturers were ultimately responsible for what the contractors did and should not contract out work to those who violated the laws. Naturally, McClintock refused to take responsibility for the contractors. She declared that she simply had a market relationship with them; what they did was not her concern. But the women thought otherwise. Through newspaper ads (which brought in thousands of dollars of contributions, along with letters of protest to the designer from consumers outraged to learn that the workers got about $5 for making a $175 dress) and direct actions such as boycotts and picketing of stores which sold McClintock clothing, they put considerable pressure on McClintock. With support from the ILGWU, now merged with the Amalgamated Clothing and Textile Workers Union to form a new union called the Union of Needle Trades, Industrial, and Textile Employees (UNITE), other unions, and central labor councils, a national campaign of justice for garment workers was initiated. Local governments and the U.S. Department of Labor were brought into the conflict as workers demanded that illegal sweatshop practices be prosecuted. Ultimately the workers prevailed, not only getting back lost wages, but also winning a garment workers' education fund and a hotline monitored by the Department of Labor.

Another important example of new organizing is home health care workers.[40] These women, again nearly all of color, provide home care for disabled people, usually elderly and always in poor health. The workers are hired (and discharged) directly by the consumers, but their pay comes from public social security funds. Pay is low, benefits nonexistent, and the work extremely dangerous. Home health care workers suffer very high rates of back injuries from lifting patients; when injured, ironically, they usually have no health insurance of their own.

Given the isolation in which home health care workers labor, it would seem impossible for them to organize. But the SEIU, working closely with community groups, succeeded in forming a union of these workers in Alameda County in California. First, the union began to research the industry, and discovered that a critical problem was the absence of an employer. So the union pressured the local government to create a public authority with which it could negotiate, along with a central place at which workers could register for work. Through dedication and coalition-building, the union visited thousands of workers in their homes and began to collect authorization cards. The diverse cultures of the workers necessitated the development of union sensitivity to complex family, ethnic, and communities issues. Literature had to be published in several languages, a throwback to the days of CIO organizing in the 1930s.

In July 1994, the union won a certification election, and then faced the equally difficult problem of collective bargaining for a large group of isolated and dissimilar workers. One of the achievements of the organizing so far has been the establishment of centers for home care workers, under the direction of a collaboration between SEIU and the nonprofit Labor Project for Working Women. Longtime union leader Ruth Needleman describes the working of the center as follows:

> The workers' centers will be run by home care workers. Designed as neighborhood union centers, they will sponsor social as well as work and union-oriented activities. A "job co-op" will match workers to jobs at a local level to enhance the referrals of the job registry. A health clinic in East Oakland will volunteer monthly health screenings at the centers.
>
> The plan includes dances, bingo, immigration and legal advice, and a day each week when union members can meet with a union steward at the center. To take advantage of the "job co-op" or other services, workers will have to volunteer time, for which they will receive points. Points are needed for services. The idea for this exchange came from the United Farm Workers (UFW) centers that required workers to contribute time for assistance.[41]

GAY AND LESBIAN WORKERS

Despite the stereotype that most gays and lesbians are privileged, the fact is that most are working people who face intense discrimination, irrespective of their race or sex. Because they are not protected by our civil rights laws, it is legal for employers to fire them simply because they are gay or lesbian. To avoid this, as well as to avoid harassment by co-workers, many gay and lesbian workers feel compelled to keep their sexual orientation secret. Unions historically have not taken the lead in creating work environments in which gay and lesbian workers could feel secure enough to come out.

The great Stonewall uprising of 1969, in which gay bar patrons in New York City fought back against police harrassment, helped to change this. Gays and lesbians began to organize openly to an unprecedented degree, and some of this activity spilled over into workplaces. Gay and lesbian caucuses have been formed within some unions, and organizations specifically devoted to gay and lesbian workplace issues have been started. Gay rights groups have also begun to agitate for workplace reforms. Some real gains have been won. It is much more common now for collective bargaining agreements to include "sexual orientation" as one of the worker characteristics against which the employer cannot discriminate, thus conferring to unionized gay and lesbian workers the same protection that the civil rights laws give to other workers. Some employers have begun to grant bereavement leave to gays and lesbians, of special importance to those who have lost friends and lovers to AIDS. Health benefits are now sometimes available to domestic partners, not just spouses. Openly gay and lesbian workers have begun to run for union office and have actually won in a few cases.

The more activity spearheaded by gay and lesbian workers within the labor movement, the more sensitive will labor become to them and the more allies they will win. The AFL-CIO has recently welcomed a gay and lesbian organization, "Pride at Work," as an officially affiliated organization. Of course, this does not mean that the labor movement has fully embraced its gay and lesbian brothers and sisters; there is still widespread discrimination. But it is a step in the right direction, one upon which future victories can be built. When AFL-CIO Vice President Linda Chavez-Thompson gives a speech, she routinely welcomes her audience by including all workers—black, white, and Hispanic, men and women, gay and straight. This may be small and symbolic, but it is impossible to imagine George Meany or Lane Kirkland doing it.[42]

WHAT COLLECTIVE BARGAINING HAS WON

Collective bargaining has been an important vehicle through which minority and female workers can win justice. As former ILGWU officer Susan Cowell said in connection with female workers who must balance the demands of both job and family,

> Labor's long-held goals are truly pro-family because they demand that the workplace and society accommodate workers as people—as members of families and communities, not merely as factors of production. Thus, while the market-place rewards productivity, unions insist on protecting workers during nonproductive periods. Union contracts provide sick leave, disability, health insurance, pensions, seniority, and job security, which are intended to protect the incomes of individuals and their families throughout the life cycle, particularly in periods of vulnerability. This principle is just as important for women who are trying to combine work and family obligations as it always has been for the traditional male breadwinner.[43]

What Cowell says can also be applied to labor's fight to shorten the hours of work. The fact that women still face a "double day" of both wage and household labor makes the struggle for shorter hours (for the same level of take-home pay) especially important for them.

In addition to the general advantages of collective bargaining, there are many ways in which collective bargaining can address the unique needs of minority and female workers. Unions can themselves practice affirmative action to insure that minorities and women are encouraged to fill union offices at all levels.[44] Affirmative action can take the form of mandatory appointments to some shop steward positions or rules for the composition of national executive boards.[45] Collective bargaining agreements can contain "no discrimination" clauses which go beyond the civil rights laws to protect workers from discrimination because of sexual orientation and marital status. As was the case for the United Packinghouse Workers, these clauses can specify that employers must hire in a nondiscriminatory way, and the union can set up special committees to see to it that anti-discrimination clauses are enforced. The idea is, in effect, to read the civil rights laws into the agreement. An arbitrator may then be inclined to use the ways in which the laws have been interpreted as guides. For example, if a black worker discharged for fighting could show that white workers caught fighting were not as likely to be fired, the discharged worker could use a *disparate impact argument* to win the case.

Affirmative action, including quotas, can be mandated for all training and apprenticeship programs run by the union or jointly with the employer. Unions also have education departments which can make the issues of racism and sexism central to their efforts, again following the lead of unions like the UPWA. Shop stewards can be trained to enforce the anti-discrimination clause by making the appropriate information requests from the employer (hirings, promotions, etc., by race and by sex) and educating the members so they are encouraged to file grievances.

There are many provisions which unions have negotiated that are of special interest to women, including, of course, women of color.[46] These include:

• **Parental leave:** This gives a parent the right to take a leave upon the birth (or adoption) of a child. Unlike the rights guaranteed parents under contracts and laws in Europe, these leaves are usually unpaid, but they do allow the parent to return to work with no loss of seniority, wage rate, and so forth. Some unions have extended these leaves to cover care for sick family members, and some contracts continue health benefits during the leave.

• **Child care:** Some agreements provide for affordable daycare in facilities on the employer's premises or in a nearby facility. In the early 1980s, ILGWU garment workers in New York City's Chinatown won daycare after a protracted struggle which involved the employers and the city, which provided a building.[47] Other contracts subsidize some of the employee's daycare expenses, while still others allow employees to contribute money to a tax-exempt account, which is used to pay for daycare.

• **Alternative work schedules:** These arrangements give employees some control over their hours and days of work and also include provisions which allow two people to, in effect, share a job. Unions have been somewhat leery of these because, in the case of four ten-hour instead of five eight-hour days, for example, the gains have to be weighed against the dangers of long days and the erosion of overtime clauses.

• **Sexual harassment:** We know now, without a doubt, that women are routinely harassed in their workplaces, either through direct touching, threats of job loss unless sexual favors are granted, and the like, or through the creation of a sexually intimidating working environment. Contracts are more likely now than they were even in the recent past to include clauses which make sexual harassment a contract violation. Some have provisions which allow for special handling of any resulting grievance, and some provide for regular training of employers and bargaining unit members.[48]

• **Health and safety:** Women's jobs subject them to a variety of health hazards, and collective bargaining agreements are beginning to address these. For example, women clerical workers must sit in front of video display terminals (VDTs) for hours every day and in doing so risk serious health problems. A contract between the Ontario Public Service Employee Union and the provincial government devotes an entire page to VDT health issues.[49]

POLITICS OF LIBERATION

Because the nature of our economic system makes it impossible for working people to liberate themselves through labor unions alone, political action is also necessary, especially for female and minority workers. Here the peculiar political trajectory of the U.S. labor movement, namely its rejection of a labor party and purging of its leftist members, has been most damaging. Sexism and racism are so deeply rooted in our society that nothing short of mass political movements, complete with civil disobedience and direct confrontations with authority, have any chance of victory in eradicating them. Such movements did develop, but organized labor was not in the forefront of them. As a consequence, the civil rights and women's movements have not had a strong enough labor component to deal a decisive blow against sexism and racism in the workplace. The absence of organized labor from the early struggles weakened the civil rights victories, and middle-class women are often blind to the issues facing working-class women.[50] No labor movement in this nation can succeed unless it challenges racial and gender inequality consistently. Had the labor movement made opposition to racism and sexism paramount many years ago, it is doubtful that the dismantling of the welfare state which we are now witnessing could have occurred.

What workers of all sexes, races, religions, and ethnicities have in common is that they are workers—by definition subordinate to their employers, who see them as the source of profits, status, and power. If working people are to have good lives, the power of their employers must be directly confronted and weakened. For this to happen, workers must act collectively, as workers. Differences of sex and race must be set aside and ultimately seen for what they are—artificial barriers to collective action. Where else are such differences as likely to be dealt with and overcome as in a labor movement? What other movements have the egalitarian potential of the labor movement? Despite its historical racism and sexism, the labor movement still offers the best hope of achieving a society without the subordination of one group to another, precisely because it aims to abolish the exploitation of the vast majority of people, those in the working class. The goal must be to remake the labor movement so as to represent what W. E. B. DuBois said about the early CIO: "the greatest and most effective effort toward interracial understanding among the working masses."

CHAPTER SEVEN

THE TASKS AHEAD

What has this book established?

• Unions have been permanent features of capitalist economies. Given the inherent conflict between workers and their employers, workers in most workplaces band together informally to improve their circumstances. However, unions provide workers with a more permanent and formal power at work.

• Unions benefit workers in many ways. Unionization has a positive independent effect on the wages and benefits of employees. Unions also give workers a voice in workplace decisions. Unions benefit all workers and not just those who are organized. Higher wages stimulate spending in the overall economy and this leads to more employment. Unions reduce inequality in incomes and fight for things beneficial to all workers, such as unemployment compensation and universal health care. Nonunion employers frequently raise wages and provide workers with some voice just to avoid unionization.[1]

• Unions in the United States usually operate under the provisions of the National Labor Relations Act (or some similar federal or state statute). As amended and interpreted by the NLRB and the courts, the act makes it difficult to organize workers. However, unions which utilize aggressive organizing models can succeed in organizing workers and build strong unions despite the law. Unions can also be organized outside of the act, and some unions have begun to do so.

• In the United States, workers are organized in numerous national (or international) unions. These unions charter local affiliates and most member activity occurs within these locals. The relationship between the locals and the national union can vary a great deal. Locals within a certain geographical area may form a central labor council, the activities of which also vary widely; some engage in organizing and coalition building, while others confine themselves to participating in local charities and getting the labor vote out at election time. Most (but by no means all) of the national unions in the United States belong to a federation of unions, the AFL-CIO, which lobbies nationally, helps fund the central labor councils, conducts an Organizing Institute to train labor organizers, does labor-related research, helps to coordinate relationships between the national unions, and so forth. The extent of democracy at all levels of the labor movement varies considerably, from the autocracy of some construction unions to the rank-and-file control of the UE.

• One primary function of a union is collective bargaining. Bargaining should be viewed as an extension of organizing and conducted as a militant and democratic campaign utilizing escalating pressure tactics, including work-to-rule, strikes, picketing, corporate campaigns, and civil disobedience. Collective bargaining agreements represent truces in the war between capital and labor. These agreements are very diverse, but any agreement can be analyzed in terms of its provisions for union security and management rights, the wage and effort bargain, individual security, and contract administration.

• Unions alone can achieve many things for their members, but there are some aspects of the working life which must be addressed politically. Unlike their counterparts in most of the rest of the world, unions in the United States have adopted a narrowly defined politics. Instead of rooting themselves in an independent political movement with working class goals, U.S. unions have practiced what labor leaders call a "pragmatic" politics. In practice, this has meant limiting their role to that of a pressure group within the Democratic Party, trying to get pro-labor politicians elected, and lobbying to get pro-worker legislation enacted. The international politics of organized labor in the United States has often been little different from that of the U.S. State Department: as a result, the AFL-CIO has not shown solidarity with most of the world's labor movements and has actually strongly supported U.S. economic and military dominance—in short, imperialism.

• The U.S. labor movement at its best has shown that it is possible to overcome the deepest divisions within the working class, most notably those of race and sex. Unfortunately, it has not always been at its best, and U.S. history is filled with examples of worker and union racism and sexism, which have badly weakened the labor movement. Despite this checkered record, unions and the labor movement may offer the majority of minority and women workers their best opportunity for liberation from their oppressive work lives and demeaned social and political circumstances.

THE DIFFICULTIES LABOR FACES

The United States has offered mixed blessings to its working men and women. On the one hand, workers have considerable political freedom, though for African Americans, gays and lesbians, and women, this was gained only after protracted, sometimes violent, struggle. But, "rags to riches" stories to the contrary, working people have seldom enjoyed sustained periods of prosperity. U.S. workers face the ups and downs of the business cycle, constantly buffeted by recessions and depressions, some of the greatest severity. But in very few other countries have employers enjoyed such a free hand in their drive to accumulate wealth. From the 1830s to 1930s, for example, the nation's labor laws put workers completely at the mercy of their employers. During these same one hundred years, virtually no social safety net existed, so that if a person could not work and had no wealth, he or she faced starvation. Further, the prevailing ideology glorified the same individualism and selfishness which led to such distressing working class conditions in the first place. To fail in the competitive struggle marked one as unfit for survival; you had only yourself to blame for your conditions, whatever they might be. Compounding this exploitation was the great diversity of the working class, differences which could be used by employers to divide workers. So English workers might hate their Irish brethren; Protestants might despise Catholics; men might feel threatened by women and brutalize and harass them; most white workers defined themselves in part by the fact that they were not black; and gays and lesbians were stigmatized and persecuted almost universally.

Yet despite the tremendous odds against them, workers did fight back, building up their unions in good times, losing ground in hard times, but keeping the memory of their successes alive to inspire their children. Periodically, in times of deep economic depression, workers rebelled against their employers and demanded radical changes. Out of all of these patient efforts and sporadic upheavals arose the two preeminent U.S. labor organizations, the AFL and the CIO. The AFL was rooted in the culture of skilled laborers, who formed narrow craft unions and to a large extent came to use the skills and the homogeneity of the members' race (white), sex (male), and culture (collective and democratic) to organize themselves and extract from their employers higher wages, shorter hours, and respect for their power. To avoid political factionalism, the AFL espoused Samuel Gompers's "reward our friends and punish our enemies" political philosophy, rejecting a more radical politics and opposition to the wage labor system.

The CIO, emerging out of upheavals during the Great Depression (built on the organizing legacies of the Knights of Labor, the Wobblies, the Socialists, and the Communists), had its base in the heterogeneous mass-production workers who toiled in our mines, mills, and factories. By the end of the Second World War, the CIO unions were a force to be reckoned with, and over the next thirty years, they helped industrial workers to achieve a level of economic security unprecedented in the nation's history. I grew up in a union household during this period and can attest to the benefits which industrial unionism brought: a house, a car, occasional vacations, family stability, and college educations for some of the children. The unions also brought profound changes in relationships inside of factories where management held uncontestable power. At the same time, the industrial unions helped to break down some of the differences between men and women and between white and black workers—if not always in social life, then at least in terms of wages, benefits, and jobs. Finally, the CIO unions helped to democratize the larger society by providing workers with a vehicle through which they could influence the politics of the nation. The recognition of universal economic rights, such as health care, social security, and unemployment insurance, owes a great deal to the labor movement.

Unfortunately, the hopes and promises engendered in the heady days of the 1930s and early 1940s were aborted. In 1955 the CIO merged with the unrepentantly exclusionary and conservative AFL to form the AFL-CIO under the leadership of a former plumber from an all-white local, George Meany. Perhaps the future looked bright because union density was close to its highest level ever and the economy was near the beginning of a long wave of growth. But we can see now that labor's optimism at the time of the merger was unwarranted. First, union density, the fraction of those employed who are in unions, began to fall in the mid-1950s, declining from 35 percent in 1955 to 23 percent in 1980. The Reagan years brought more precipitous declines, with density at about 14.9 percent in 1996. In the private sector, density is a mere 10.3 percent, not much higher than at the beginning of the Great Depression. In the public sector, density is a more robust 37.7 percent, so it is clear that without tremendous growth in public sector unionization, the labor movement would be much weaker.[2] Declining densities have become so marked that absolute union membership has fallen as well; while in 1983 union membership was 17.7 million, in 1995 it was only 16.4 million.[3] Once proud unions have witnessed catastrophic losses of members and have begun to merge with one another to stop the bleeding.[4] Between the year in which each union's membership was at its peak and the year 1995, the UAW lost 509,000 members, the Carpenters 372,000, and the Steelworkers 659,000.[5] A few unions have gained members, but this has sometimes been wholly or partly the result of mergers with other unions.

Second, the low and declining union densities in the United States are all the more troubling when they are compared with those in other advanced capitalist economies. In Scandinavia, densities are between 60 and 80 percent. In the rest of Europe, they are not as high, but for the most part they are much higher than in the United States—40 percent in Great Britain and 33 percent in Germany, for example. In France, density is only 10 percent, but unions have a much stronger position there than here, as demonstrated by the ability of a few public sector unions to shut down much of the economy.[6] In Canada, density is around 30 percent and has not fallen as precipitously as here. Even in New Zealand, which has undergone a profoundly anti-labor political restructuring, density is at 23 percent.[7] It would be misleading to imply that the United States is unique in suffering union density losses, because organized labor has been losing ground nearly everywhere in the world. However, the situation in the United States is certainly among the worst.

Third, the political achievements of our labor movement have been pretty meager, especially if measured against those of many other movements. The AFL-CIO was unable to stop or even slow down the reactionary policies of the Reagan-Bush era, policies which were, incredibly, supported by the largest U.S. union, the Teamsters (before its corrupt regime was swept aside by union reformers).[8] The U.S. social welfare system always paled in comparison to those in Western Europe and Scandinavia.[9] Americans do not have universal health care. The U.S. unemployment compensation system is extremely porous, covering less than one-half of the unemployed.[10] The United States does not have comprehensive training and retraining programs for its young people or those displaced by corporate restructuring, and it has the highest level of inequality of wealth and income of any advanced capitalist country.[11] Visitors from abroad are shocked at the extent and depth of the poverty which marks U.S. inner cities. Now the social welfare system is being dismantled, not just at the insistence of Republicans but at the initiative of Democrats supported by organized labor.

REASONS FOR LABOR'S DECLINE: EXTERNAL FORCES

Many reasons have been offered for the decline of the U.S. labor movement, by analysts both inside and outside of organized labor. Much of the discussion portrays unions as victims of external forces over which they have had little control.[12] It is instructive to look at these arguments, because, while each contains some truth, taken as a whole they are not compelling.

First, it is argued that the shift away from production of goods and toward services has inevitably led to a reduction in union density. This is because a higher fraction of workers are unionized in the goods-producing industries than in those which produce services. Other things equal, this shift lowers the union density. Of course, there must be some truth to this because the shift has, in fact, occurred. Yet it cannot be the whole truth because densities have also fallen *within* the goods-producing industries, for example, in coal-mining, steel, and automobiles. Furthermore, this argument begs the question: why is density so low in the service sector? There is nothing inevitable about this.

Service workers are highly organized in the Scandinavian countries. If bank tellers, clerks in stores, secretaries, janitors, and building guards can be organized there, why not here?

Second, the proposition is advanced that workers in the United States have a low and declining demand for the services which labor unions provide. This may be because U.S. workers still believe that they can move into a higher economic class through their own efforts. Or it may be because employers have provided workers with enough voice and good enough wages and benefits to make workers believe that a union wouldn't do them much good. There are many problems with this argument. Polls indicate that a much higher number of employees would like to have a union at their place of employment than are currently in unions. The gap between desire and reality is greatest for minority workers, who overwhelmingly favor unionization, and these are the very workers whose share of future employment will increase. According to the polls, the willingness of workers to vote for a union has been declining, but this could just as well be a consequence of labor's decline as a cause of it. That is, workers might choose to join strong and democratic unions, if given the option, but when they express disinterest to pollsters, they have in mind the weak and often bureaucratic unions that now exist.

Third, it is claimed that capital is now so mobile, especially internationally, that employers can easily subvert unionization attempts by moving their plants to places like Mexico, where wage rates are much lower than they are here. This mobility is largely the product of the electronics revolution, as well as the tendency of employers to use unskilled labor whenever possible. Capital is now so "global" that, barring the immediate development of an international labor movement, labor unions in any one place are doomed to fail. Insurance companies in the United States can have their paperwork done in Central America and transmitted back home by computer. General Motors can open a plant in Mexico, and because of its advanced electronic technology, suffer no loss of worker productivity. Such arguments have been made so often, by persons of all political persuasions, that they are typically taken as articles of faith. Yet the evidence in favor of them is surprisingly weak. Many service-sector operations cannot be moved at all; a McDonald's or nursing home cannot be moved to Mexico City and still serve customers in L.A. Further, capital in most industries is not instantly mobile, and in many industries capital prefers to locate close to major markets. Since most sales are still in the advanced capitalist countries, business typically prefers to be located in them. Thus most manufacturing, presumably the sector most likely to move to poor, low-wage nations, is still located in advanced capitalist economies. Finally, a good deal of the capital mobility (capital in the form of money and in physical equipment) which does take place is the result of political decisions made by governments influenced (if not ruled) by the owners of capital, and not the result of inevitable and inexorable technological change. Governments make trade agreements and tax laws which encourage corporations to locate just across the border in Mexico. Governments are responsible for the lack of environmental protection laws which lower the cost of production and encourage capital export. Governments have eliminated the controls which they once had over the flow of money across national borders; there is no reason why such controls cannot be resurrected.

A fourth suspect in labor's decline is the harsh legal climate in which unions must function.[13] There is no doubt that our labor laws favor the employer in both union organizing campaigns and collective bargaining. Employers are free to campaign aggressively against unions, and can disseminate anti-union messages even if they are false. Employers can hold mandatory captive audience meetings in the workplace, but unions have no right to respond in the workplace. Union organizers who are not employees have no right to be on the employer's property, but an employer is free to hire a union-busting consultant and have its staff on the premises every day. Supervisors have no legal protection if they refuse to participate in the employer's anti-union campaign. Many employers engage in illegal practices, such as firing or otherwise discriminating against union supporters, because they know that the penalties for doing so are pitifully small. In collective bargaining, the penalty for an employer bargaining in bad faith is usually simply an order from the NLRB to return to the bargaining table. An employer suffers no monetary penalty for bad-faith bargaining, so is it any wonder that employers routinely refuse to reach agreement with the unions representing their employees? If the workers strike, it is legal for the employer to hire permanent replacements, and many companies have done so.

It must be noted that the original National Labor Relations Act, enacted in 1935, was more protective of workers' rights than is now the case. The original law has been amended several times, and each amendment has strengthened the hand of the employers. The Taft-Hartley amendments of 1947, for example, prohibited the use of most "secondary" actions by labor unions. Thus, it is now illegal for workers to picket the sites of employers other than their own, a tactic that is often necessary to pressure an unfair employer's weak points. Taft-Hartley also prohibits one group of workers from striking in sympathy with another group. Similarly, the early National Labor Relations Board was much more inclined to see its job as enforcing the rights of workers to form and join labor unions and to engage in concerted struggles against their employers. More recently, with some exceptions, the NLRB has been more sympathetic to employers; the board under Reagan pretty much abdicated its legal responsibilities to workers. The consequences have been a rapid increase in unfair labor practices and a sharp reduction in the rate at which unions win certification elections.[14]

There is no doubt that changes in the laws have been responsible for some of labor's collapse since the peak period of union density in the mid-1950s. However, two points need to be kept in mind. First, it is possible to win union certification elections despite the law, provided that unions use the tactics described in this book. It is also possible to force an employer to recognize a union without using the NLRB at all, again using the same weapons combined with direct actions. In Las Vegas, for example, unions have used mass picketing, demonstrations, boycotts, strikes, and civil disobedience to force the big hotels to recognize their employees' unions. Similar tactics were used by West Coast janitors, in their famous "Justice for Janitors" campaign to win recognition from the owners of the big office buildings which they clean.[15] Additionally, one must ask why were the labor laws changed in the first place, and why are they so weakly enforced? Could it be that organized labor's own weakness is itself responsible? If so, the effect has been confused with the cause.

A final, and very common, explanation offered for the union movement's growing weakness is the initiation of an anti-union "corporate agenda" sometime in the early 1970s.[16] According to one version of this argument, a "labor-management" accord was reached after the Second World War.[17] Top corporate leadership came to accept the inevitability of unions and agreed to bargain collectively with them over a range of wages, hours, and terms and conditions of employment. In return, the unions agreed not to interfere in the management of the businesses (which is reflected in the "management rights" clauses which appear in nearly all agreements) and to refrain from striking during the contract period (thus the "no strike" clauses found in nearly all contracts). Both parties benefitted greatly from this accord, as corporations prospered and workers enjoyed rising real wages and improved benefits. When the long postwar boom ended sometime in the early 1970s, as a result of overproduction and growing international competition, what once seemed inevitable began to seem dispensable. As corporate profit rates fell, employers found the accord more and more onerous and began to look for a way out. This took the form of the "corporate agenda": an all-out offensive against organized labor, including massive plant closings, the creation of anti-labor lobbying groups, a greater willingness to endure (or even encourage) strikes and hire permanent replacements for strikers, and a thorough propaganda campaign against organized labor. The agenda reached fruition with the election of Ronald Reagan as president in 1980. Reagan fired the air traffic controllers and appointed corporate lackeys to the NLRB, the Occupational Safety and Health Administration (OSHA), and many other agencies whose job, presumably, was to protect workers' rights.

The AFL-CIO endorses the "corporate agenda" argument, often portraying itself as a victim of corporate irresponsibility and greed. In the AFL-CIO pamphlet *America Needs a Raise,* one goal for renewal is to "persuade employers to practice corporate responsibility for their employees and the communities they serve as well as for their stockholders and executives. . . ."[18] In other words, labor is urging capital to return to the "accord," ending the "corporate agenda."

There are many problems with this last explanation for labor's demise. The fall in union density began before the early 1970s. What accounts for this earlier decline? Capital was busy undermining the "accord" long before this period. Throughout the postwar boom, employers were busy introducing labor-saving machinery, greatly reducing their reliance on union labor. They were continuously using the time-management principles of Frederick Taylor to de-skill work, making union workers easily replaceable.[19] They were expanding and moving their operations to nonunion parts of the United States and to foreign countries. In other words, corporations were violating the "accord" even its heyday. In my hometown, the critical year was 1958, when the Pittsburgh Plate Glass Company (now PPG Industries) defeated the union in a long strike and began to open plants in low-wage, rural, and nonunion areas, introducing a new method of making plate glass which spelled the doom of the union plants. The end of the long postwar boom merely produced a *culmination* of the corporate agenda, the makings of which had existed all along.

REASONS FOR LABOR'S DECLINE: INTERNAL FORCES

In the early 1970s, when the labor-corporate "accord" ended, most unions were run by officers not elected by democratic vote of the rank and file. They were staffed by people appointed by these officers. The top officers were very well paid, lived and associated with people in similar circumstances, and seldom faced the risk of being unseated by insurgent forces. Collective bargaining was a highly centralized affair, far removed from the control of the workers, who seldom participated in negotiations or even grievance processing.[20] Few unions contained organized oppositions, and it was a rare union which afforded its members a formal democratic system of due process whenever the incumbent leaders decided that a member had behaved in a manner critical of the leadership. Even the best unions, such as the United Auto Workers, could be described as "one-party states" with new leaders chosen (anointed might be a better word) by the old. The worst unions, such as the Teamsters and many construction unions, were run as dictatorships, complete with ruthless violence against anyone who dared to complain, and were infiltrated by criminal elements, who routinely raided union treasuries to finance casinos and other underworld ventures. When Joseph "Jock" Yablonski, a former officer of the United Mine Workers, organized a reformist challenge, the union's president, Tony Boyle, actually had Yablonski murdered.[21]

Still, at the local level, thousands of unions operated in a reasonably democratic way, vigorously negotiating contracts, enforcing agreements, and investigating grievances. National unions won many good things for their members, including decent pensions and longer vacations. Central labor councils helped to elect many decently liberal members of Congress. The AFL-CIO continued to support policies which were, for the most part, in the interest of the working class. But even at their best, unions practiced what Kim Moody calls the "servicing model" of unionism.[22] That is, each union saw its main function as servicing its existing membership: getting the members more money and benefits and policing the collective bargaining agreements. This approach, in turn, meant that unions spent little money and used minimal personnel to organize new locals. Today the average union spends a scant 3 percent of its budget on organizing; in some cases more money is spent on the union's annual convention than on organizing.[23] Notwithstanding the external forces working against them, how did unions expect to defend their members when they devoted almost no attention to organizing the unorganized? Some union leaders, including former AFL-CIO president George Meany, professed a lack of interest in nonunion workers, implying that these people were somehow responsible for their lack of union representation.[24]

There were other serious problems with organized labor during the years of the "accord." By ceding control over the workplaces to the employers, unions ignored the fact that even though workers wanted and enjoyed the higher wages won during this period, working conditions are also critical to workers' well-being. Employers continued to intensify the pace of work and to deny workers a meaningful say in how the work was done. Autoworkers may have earned high wages, but they were physically and emotionally tested by the numbing monotony of work along a high-speed assembly line.[25] Unions hesitated to deal with immediate workplace problems directly as they had often done in the past, and instead told workers to file grievances. The union's job was to enforce the contract, including the "no-strike" agreement. On another level, the labor movement was thoroughly enmeshed in the politics of the Democratic Party, which is beholden to corporate funding. It would take a remarkably naive person to believe that this is the party of the working man and woman. Yet labor did the Democrats' bidding, and internationally served the interests of U.S. corporations by allying itself with the CIA and State Department. How could a labor movement serve the interests of the working class if it was completely integrated into the politics of the very "corporate agenda" which many now blame for the woeful state of working America?

Take note that the labor-management "accord" began during the same period in which the left-wing unions and radical unionists responsible for the birth and growth of the CIO were being systematically purged from the labor movement. The severing of the labor movement from the left had disastrous consequences, because labor radicalism has always been essential for workers' advances. Would employers have been so willing to recognize and bargain with the AFL unions had not Debs and the rest of the militants nearly brought the house of capital to its knees? Would the CIO unions have survived without the efforts of the radicals who confronted the employers everywhere in the nation?

The successes of the radicals in mobilizing masses of workers during these periods did not come from "service" unionism or alliance with the Democratic Party. They came from the ability of radicals to infuse workers with a vision of a better society—where workers had rights, had some control over their lives; a society in which they were more than factors of production. According to this vision, people stuck together as a matter of principle, irrespective of their sex or race. Furthermore, for the labor left, organizing workers was only the beginning. Once organized, their unions would be democratic and militant. Collective bargaining agreements would not be ends in themselves but one of many means, including direct actions, to continuously deepen and strengthen worker power on the job. Politically, the left-led unions would fight as independently as they could for those things which would make workers stronger: full employment, progressive taxes, an end to militarism and empire, and support for public investment in health, education, and welfare, and solidarity with workers around the world.

We have been led to believe that the radical unions of the CIO were mere dupes of the Soviet Union and more interested in promoting its interests than in building a democratic working class movement. However, modern research is showing that this is an errant point of view.[26] Whatever their weaknesses (and often a knee-jerk reverence for the Communist states was one of them), the left-wing unions won better contracts than most of their competitors, contracts which gave more power to the rank and file. Furthermore, these unions were often among the most democratic in the labor movement, and they were the biggest thorns in the sides of the employers.[27] In those unions controlled by more conservative elements, the radicals, sometimes organized as formal caucuses, provided a constant challenge to the leaders to take stronger positions than they otherwise might have taken. Most remarkably, the left prompted the unions to make more progress toward ending racial (and to some extent sexual) discrimination than any other organizations in the history of the country. After the Second World War, the CIO began "Operation Dixie" to organize workers in the low-wage and racist South. Unfortunately, the war against the left had already begun, dooming this critical movement to failure. Had the left been allowed to lead this movement, and had it been supported as strongly as, say, the UMW supported the CIO in the late 1930s, the entire postwar history of the United States might have been dramatically altered.[28] Had the CIO retained its radical core, it might have at least won the enviable social welfare state won by the Scandinavian unions during the same era. To its shame, the CIO ended up in bed with the AFL. Instead of standing up to the cold warriors of both political parties and the AFL, instead of fighting McCarthyism and the witch-hunts of the 1950s, the CIO threw out its best and brightest and doomed the labor movement to the "corporate agenda." Some workers got more money and moved to the suburbs, but the labor movement, the movement for social justice, died, and with that death came the opportunity to roll back working-class living standards.

THE "NEW VOICE"

George Meany, with his ubiquitous cigar and rough New York accent, was at least colorful. His successor, Lane Kirkland, like Meany a career labor function-ary, was dull and totally incapable of developing a strategy to confront the "corporate agenda." While business was beating up on workers, the AFL-CIO in the 1970s and 1980s preached labor-management cooperation, trying to resurrect the "accord." But the "accord" was the product of special circum-stances. Workers prospered during the postwar boom because the economy grew rapidly, and enough of them were organized to make it worthwhile for employers to bargain with their unions rather than go on the offensive. By the time Kirkland took office, corporations were preaching cooperation but en-gaging in a no-holds-barred class war. As union density plummeted and total membership also began to fall, it became clear to some within the AFL-CIO that fundamental changes were needed. In many unions, rank-and-file groups, sometimes led by a new group of radicals who had come of age during the tumultuous 1960s, formed and pushed sclerotic leadership bodies to do something to stop the assault on working-class living standards.[29] The Teamsters for a Democratic Union (TDU) is perhaps the most famous of these organizations, and deservedly so.

The reform movement in the national unions eventually reached the AFL-CIO itself. In the early 1990s, pressure was put on Kirkland to resign. At first he refused, and when he ultimately did resign, he hoped that his anointed successor and interim president, Tom Donahue, would be able to stave off the reformers and keep power in the hands of the old guard. But it was too late. A reform slate, the "New Voice," contested the election of officers at the 1995 AFL-CIO convention in New York City, the first contested election in one hundred years. The New Voice candidates were John Sweeney, president of the growing and innovative Service Employees International Union (creator of the *Contract Campaign Manual*), Richard Trumka, militant president of the United Mine Workers, and Linda Chavez-Thompson, a dynamic Chicana local leader out of the American Federation of State, County, and Municipal Employees (AFSCME). The New Voice slate convincingly defeated the Donahue forces and began to implement their programs, which, they said, would build a new social movement to challenge the corporate agenda.

Since their election, the New Voice leaders have done some remarkable things, and, in the process, have helped to give new life to the labor movement. Sweeney has made organizing the prime focus of the AFL-CIO. The AFL-CIO's Organizing Institute is training new organizers and encouraging the use of the sort of confrontational tactics described in this book. Director of Organizing Richard Bensinger has refreshingly stated, "We will be successful only to the degree that we recognize our own responsibility for our own failures."[30] During the past few years, the AFL-CIO has conducted a "Union Summer," in which young people, mostly college students, are trained to participate in organizing campaigns. The success of this program has led to the start of a "Union Senior" counterpart.[31] Sweeney is encouraging member unions to devote 30 percent of their budgets to organizing, and while not many unions are at this level, some are spending more money on organizing. The AFL-CIO has also created a Working Women's Department, headed by Karen Nussbaum, the former director of the women's organizing group, 9 to 5. Women workers have been polled throughout the country to help unions get a better handle on women's issues. Sweeney hopes to build bridges with women's organizations as well as many other interest groups who might be labor's "natural allies."[32] Cities across the country are being declared "union cities," and plans are being made to rejuvenate and support their central labor councils in spearheading the organizing of new unions.

The AFL-CIO sponsored a study of the nation's central labor councils, and it discovered that some of these were already organizing, some even helping to build broad-based social movements. Since central labor councils are tied directly to the AFL-CIO, they can become good vehicles for funding and organizing somewhat independently of the national unions, over which the AFL-CIO has no immediate control. These bodies can also encourage their member unions to cooperate in organizing. If one union does exceptional organizing in an area, it can help to organize any group of workers, even if they would typically be organized by another union. Or unions can develop joint organizing campaigns. If it seems best to organize all of the workers in a town or region at once and together, the central labor council can lead the organizing drive itself. Labor councils can also be important focal points for the creation of broader social movement groups, such as the one built in Atlanta to secure high-paying jobs at the last Olympics. There are already in existence labor-based groups, such as Black Workers for Justice, which have done good work in organizing, and the central labor councils can join with these and perhaps provide, via the AFL-CIO, critical funding.[33]

To their great credit, the New Voice officers have begun to dismantle the AFL-CIO's International Affairs Department. According to journalist Marc Cooper, "A new Corporate Affairs Department will coordinate national and international actions, including 'corporate campaigns,' against targeted employers. As an added bonus this new department has eaten up much of the office space occupied until recently by the federation's notorious cold-war fighting International Department. . . ."[34] Hopefully, this will mark the beginning of a new era in international solidarity. Some member unions, and the independent UE, have participated in cross-border organizing to help Mexican workers confront the transnational corporations located along the U.S.-Mexico border and to build independent unions.[35] Recently the AFL-CIO hosted, for the first time, representatives of the world's "international trade secretariats," organizations which represent unions worldwide in various economic sectors, such as metals, construction, and communications.[36] These secretariats help to coordinate the actions of unions in each particular sector around the world. When the United Steel Workers went after the union-busting Ravenswood Aluminum Corporation, it asked for and got tremendous help from the secretariats and European labor unions.[37]

In 1980, the AFL-CIO stood by while Reagan fired the air traffic controllers. These days the federation takes an active and sometimes aggressive stance in connection with particular labor disputes. Sweeney, Trumka, and Chavez actually go to labor hot spots and offer support; they have done this for the strawberry workers in Watsonville, California, apple harvesters in the state of Washington, and the newspaper strikers in Detroit. The AFL-CIO offered strong support to the Teamsters in the recent UPS strike. Such solidarity is important because it encourages member unions to show solidarity, too. On a more symbolic level, the federation has begun to hold its conventions in places where there is a strong working-class presence rather than in the Florida resort town of Bal Harbor.

The AFL-CIO has also made overtures to intellectuals. During the 1930s many progressive intellectuals supported and worked for the labor movement. The labor movement was the center of action for anyone interested in fundamental social change. In 1996, a teach-in on labor and intellectuals held at Columbia University in New York City attracted thousands of participants, including many prominent scholars and writers. A similar event was held at UCLA in February 1997, and a third at the University of Pittsburgh in September 1997. Such events are important because they give organized labor good publicity and lay the groundwork for recruiting college students into the labor movement. The labor movement is more open to intellectuals, even those who are openly left-wing, than it has been at any time since the 1930s and early 1940s, creating an opportunity to transcend the split between labor and the left. There are a good many leftists in the unions and in AFL-CIO staff positions, and they now can be a lot more open about their political views. In turn, the unions and the AFL-CIO are more open to the left intellectuals' analyses of their unions and of the larger society and to their suggestions for more successful organizing and bargaining. Recently, the AFL-CIO contracted with the left-leaning Center for Popular Economics in Amherst, Massachusetts for a package of materials for worker study groups in economics.[39] The eight-week course, titled *Common Sense Economics*, represents a real step forward in economic education for the AFL-CIO. Of course, the federation cannot force member unions to use the materials, and the materials themselves are not without problems, but there is no doubt that labor educators will use the course, and that the workers who take the course will encounter a more accurate view of the capitalist economic system than most ideological institutions in this society provide.

AN INTERNATIONAL LABOR MOVEMENT?

As capital has become more mobile, ceaselessly moving around the globe in search of new markets and lower costs, and as national governments have become more helpless to control this, some analysts have argued that it is no longer possible for workers in any one country to successfully challenge employers. The threat of plant closings and capital flight is indeed too great for any particular country's government or workers to challenge employers. The only hope for workers is to forge a truly international labor movement to challenge employers globally.

Workers can and must organize whenever and wherever they can. Yet while employers are increasingly flexible and mobile, most production is still domestic and much of it cannot be moved at all. National governments could place controls upon capital mobility, but they will not, unless there is a well-organized labor movement to force them to do so. It is rather foolish to believe that an international labor movement is going to suddenly emerge when unions have not been able to organize more than a tiny minority of workers here. So, for now, the main task of the U.S. labor movement must be to organize as many workers as it can and to develop an independent labor politics to build a comprehensive labor movement.

Naturally, labor in the United States must ally itself with workers in the rest of the world and do what it can to support workers' struggles everywhere. It is true that workers around the world are becoming more alike in that they face the same attacks from employers and governments. So there is a real basis for cooperation and support. It is in the interests of U.S. workers to help to raise the living standards of workers worldwide, because this reduces the ability of employers to pit one group of workers against another. And with the end of the Cold War, it is now possible to imagine that the U.S. labor movement will take off its ideological blinders and support workers' struggles in other countries irrespective of the politics of these struggles. Already we have witnessed many hopeful signs: some U.S. unions helping Mexican workers to organize; the use of electronic communications to facilitate worldwide support for various strikes, including boycotts of employer products; international coordination of collective bargaining; and so forth. American workers need to learn about efforts elsewhere. For example, Korean workers have engaged in mass agitations to win representation, as well as to assert themselves politically. Throughout Europe, the unemployed have taken to the streets, often with the support of the labor movements. Confronting employers and confronting the government more and more amount to the same thing; workers' struggles are increasingly political struggles. Further, international labor needs to coordinate its goals. For example, if workers in all countries were fighting hard for a reduction in the working day, it would be much easier for labor movements to cooperate with one another and show solidarity.[38]

STILL TO COME

This is a more hopeful time for unions and the labor movement than any time in the past thirty years. The economy has been growing strongly, and labor shortages are developing in many markets. If the public response to the UPS strikers is any indication, unions are no longer viewed as just another special interest group. For labor to be reborn, however, it must become more willing to declare its political independence. As a first step in that direction, organized labor should declare its fundamental principles.

What does the new AFL-CIO leadership see as a good society? It is difficult to know. A close inspection of *America Needs a Raise* or *Common Sense Economics* reveals little in terms of what the labor movement stands for in principle. There are a lot of words devoted to what it is against: low wages, growing inequality in income and wealth, unregulated free trade, the destruction of our social safety net, the privatization of public services, high interest rates, exorbitant CEO pay, excessive overtime, bad labor laws, a flat tax, cuts in the capital gains tax, and corporate tax breaks. But the AFL-CIO shies away from saying forthrightly what it stands *for*. It does not as a matter of course demand things which should be human rights. Brief mention is sometimes made of these things, but they are not at the center of the labor movement's program.

What organized labor lacks is a working-class ideology, a labor-centered way of thinking and acting which is based upon the understanding that a capitalist society is not and cannot be a just one. What might motivate workers to become part of a movement is the possibility that the current system can be transcended and a new, democratic, egalitarian society built.

A list of labor-centered principles that would respond to this need might look like this:

1. **Employment as a right.** Unemployment not only wastes the output that the unemployed could have produced, it also wastes human beings and leads to a large number of social problems from arrest and imprisonment to murder and suicide.

2. **Meaningful work.** Human beings have the unique ability to conceptualize work tasks and then perform them. Yet most jobs utilize only a fraction of human ability. This leads to profound alienation and a hatred of work. Instead of seeing labor as the fulfillment of our humanity, we see it as a necessary evil to be avoided if at all possible.

3. **Socialization of consumption.** We waste enormous effort to purchase goods and services which ought to be provided by society. Examples include education at all levels, health care (including care of the aged), child care, transportation, and recreation (parks, libraries, playgrounds, and gyms). It would be far more efficient to share responsibility for such public needs.

4. **Democratic control of production.** We pride ourselves on having a free society, yet nearly all workplaces are run as dictatorships. Shouldn't we have control over the production of the outputs which we depend upon for survival?

Why should the glass factory that dominated my hometown for nearly a century be able to pack up and leave without the will of the people being considered, much less being decisive?

5. Shorter hours of work. At the same time that hundreds of millions of people worldwide cannot find enough work, millions of others are working hours comparable to those worked during the industrial revolution.[39] People are working too much to enjoy life. Why should this be so?

6. An end to discrimination. What possible justification can there be for the gross inequalities in jobs, incomes, housing, and wealth that exist between those who are white and male and just about everyone else? No just society can be built on a foundation of racial, ethnic, and gender discrimination.

7. Wage and income equality. I can think of no good reason why I should earn four times as much as the men and women who clean the buildings in which I labor and teach. Would I refuse to work if they earned the same as I do? How can it be justified that a CEO makes tens of millions of dollars per year? For what? Does anyone believe that no one would do these jobs for a lot less?

What prevents our labor leaders from openly advocating these things? An anecdote will provide a proximate answer. A friend of mine was hired by an international agency to investigate how employer threats to shut down plants affect workers' ability to unionize. This study was funded largely by the AFL-CIO. The report showed that employer shutdown threats had increased markedly since the passage of NAFTA. When it appeared that the Clinton administration was putting pressure on the Department of Labor not to publish the report, my friend turned to the AFL-CIO for help. Such help was not forthcoming. It appeared that powerful forces within the AFL-CIO did not want to embarrass their good friend, Bill Clinton. Eventually the AFL-CIO apologized to the author, but not before she received a lot of heavy fire, especially after she decided to inform the press of her findings. This is a very curious situation. The AFL-CIO went all out to prevent the passage of NAFTA, and it took massive payoffs from President Clinton to get NAFTA through Congress. Yet, when a report showed NAFTA doing some of the things which opponents had predicted, some AFL-CIO leaders opposed making it public.

What is going on here? In a nutshell, business as usual for the labor movement: stay in line with the Democratic Party come hell or high water. When the CIO was formed and its militant unions were taking on the bosses, there was a strong left-wing component in the labor movement. The left-wingers helped to build unions which were among the most democratic in the country, unions which militantly confronted the employers and won some of the best contracts. What is more, the left-wingers held fast to a vision of a better society, one more democratic and egalitarian, of a world without discrimination or wars, founded upon community and solidarity. They knew that such a society could only be brought about through an independent politics, which might make provisional alliances with the traditional parties, as was the case during the New Deal. Class conscious and democratic unions, combined with progressive politics, would provide a framework within which rank-and-file workers could improve their lot in life and at the same time think about larger issues. Through these unions, it was possible for black and white workers to forcibly integrate their neighborhood bars and restaurants and for women to sometimes play leading roles. They were by no means perfect, yet these CIO unions held out promise of a great social transformation. Sadly, this was not to be. Too many labor leaders, almost all of those in the AFL unions and quite a few from CIO unions, joined hands with the cold warriors and crushed the progressive unionists. At the same time, the remaining CIO unions became firmly entrenched as very junior partners in the Democratic Party. The "accord" was about to begin, except from this perspective it looks a lot more like labor-management collaboration.

The new AFL-CIO is certainly a hopeful sign, and we are perhaps seeing the beginning of an upswing in union organizing as the New Voice team puts its organizing model into practice. However, if the AFL-CIO is to become the center of a new social movement, it will have to proclaim a more radical vision of the future than it has so far. This cannot be done unless labor embraces an independent, working-class politics. How this could happen remains to be seen. One possibility is that a statement of principles could be used as a basis for winning as many allies as possible, including political parties such as the Labor Party and New Party. Perhaps local, regional, and national meetings could be convened at which these groups would debate the principles and refine

Student volunteers in "Union Summer" join a protest against the Michigan state government's privatization policies, Lansing, 1996. [Jim West]

them, leading to a national umbrella group. The resulting organization could have the short-term goal of redefining the agenda of the major political parties, much as right-wing coalitions have done for the past thirty years.

For any of this to happen, thoughtful, effective radicals must play a part in the structures of the AFL-CIO, as well as in the national unions and central labor councils. But the kind of labor radicalization that will do the job is most dependent on the workers in locals across the country fighting to make their unions democratic. In grassroots organizing, based as it must be on rank-and-file control, in struggles for the hearts and souls of our national unions, in alliances with organizations and individuals committed to building the kind of society that is within our grasp, in battles with the employers, whose usefulness becomes less apparent each day, a new labor movement and a new social movement might be born. That is the hope for the future.

APPENDIX

USEFUL RESOURCES

Directories

C. D. Gifford, *Directory of Labor Organizations* (Washington, D.C.: The Bureau of National Affairs, 1996).

Workers' Education Local 189, *Directory of Labor Education, 1997-1998* (Hyattsville, MD: Local 189, 1997).

Handbooks and Manuals

BNA PLUS, *Source Book on Collective Bargaining: Wages, Benefits, and Other Contract Issues* (Washington, D.C.: Bureau of National Affairs, 1997).

Center for Labor Education and Research, University of Hawaii, *Labor Dispute Picketing: Organizing a Legal Picket in Hawaii* (Honolulu: Center for Labor Education and Research, n.d.).

Barry Hirsch and David A. Mcpherson, *Union Membership and Earnings Data Book* (Washington, D.C.: Bureau of National Affairs). Published annually.

Staughton Lynd, *Labor Law for the Rank and File* (Chicago: Charles H. Kerr Publishing Company, 1994).

William Puette, *Through Jaundiced Eyes: How the Media View Organized Labor* (Ithaca, NY: ILR Press, 1992).

Robert M. Schwartz, *The Legal Rights of Union Stewards* (Cambridge, MA: Work Rights Press, 1994).

Service Employees International Union, *Contract Campaign Manual* (Washington, D.C.: SEIU, 1988).

William Ury, *Getting Past No* (New York: Bantam Books, 1993).

Tom Zaniello, *Working Stiffs, Union Maids, Reds, and Riffraff: An Organized Guide to Films about Labor* (Ithaca, NY: ILR Press, 1996).

Research and Resource Providers

Bureau of National Affairs (BNA), 1231 25th St. N.W., Washington, D.C. 20037, (800) 452-7773.

Center for Popular Economics, Post Office Box 785, Amherst, MA 01004, (413) 545-0743.

Economic Policy Institute, 1660 L Street, N.W., Suite 1200, Washington, D.C. 20036, (202) 775-8810.

Labor Research Association, 145 West 28th St., New York, NY, 10001-6191, (212) 714-1677.

Organizations and Advocacy Groups

A. Philip Randolph Institute, 1444 Eye St., N.W., Third Fl., Washington, D.C. 20005, (202) 289-2774.

AFL-CIO, 815 16th St., N.W., Washington, D.C. 20006, (202) 637-5058.

AFL-CIO Organizing Institute, 1101 14th St., N.W., Suite 320, Washington, D.C. 20005, (202) 639-6200.

Asian Pacific American Labor Alliance, 1101 14th St., N.W. Suite 310, Washington, D.C. 20005, (202) 842-1263.

Association for Union Democracy (AUD), 500 State St., Brooklyn, NY 11217-1803, (718) 855-6650.

Black Workers for Justice, P.O. Box 1863, Rocky Mount, NC 27802, (919) 977-8162.

Center to Protect Workers' Rights, 111 Massachusetts Ave, N.W., Washington, D.C. 20001, (202) 962-8490.

Chinese Staff and Workers Association, P.O. Box 130401, New York, NY 10013-0995, (212) 619-7979.

Coalition of Black Trade Unionists, P.O. Box 66268, Washington, D.C. 20035-6268, (202) 429-1203.

Coalition of Labor Union Women, 1126 16th St., N.W. Washington, D.C. 20036, (202) 466-4610.

Labor/Community Strategy Center, The Wiltern Center, 3780 Wilshire Blvd., Suite 1200, Los Angeles, CA 90010, (213) 387-2800.

Labor Party, P.O. Box 53177, Washington, D.C. 20009.

Lavender Labor, c/o Patti R. Roberts, 407 North St., Oakland, CA 94609.

National Jobs for All Coalition, 475 Riverside Drive, Suite 832, New York, NY 10115-0050, (212) 870-3449.

National Mobilization Against Sweatshops (NMASS), P.O. Box 130293, New York, NY 10013-0995, (718) 633-9757.

New Party, 227 West 40th St., Suite 1303, New York, NY 10018, (212) 302-5053.

9 to 5 National Association of Working Women, 614 Superior Ave., N.W., Suite 852, Cleveland, OH 44113-1387, (216) 566-9308.

Pride at Work, P.O. Box 65893, Washington, DC 20035-5893, (202) 667-8237.

Workers Defense League, 275 Seventh Ave., New York, NY 10001, (212) 627-1931

Periodicals

Labor History, Bobst Library, Tamiment Institute, New York University, 70 Washington Square South, New York, NY 10012.

Labor Notes, 7435 Michigan Ave., Detroit, MI 48210, (313) 842-6262.

Labor's Heritage, 1000 New Hampshire Ave., Silver Spring, MD 20903. (301) 431-5457.

Monthly Labor Review, Bureau of Labor Statistics, Superintendent of Documents, Government Printing Office, Washington, D.C. 20402.

New Labor Forum, Labor Resource Center, Queens College, City University of New York, 25 W. 43rd St., 19th Floor, New York, NY 10036.

WorkingUSA, 80 Business Park Drive, Armonk, NY 10504. (800) 541-6563.

Websites

AFL-CIO: http://www.aflcio.org/unionand.htm

Canadian labor: http://www.unionnet.org/signmeup/index.html

Mexican labor: http://www.igc.apc.org/unitedelect

World labor: http://www.unicc.org/ilo

General labor: http://www.igc.apc.org/labornet
   http://jmcneil.sba.muohio.edu/unions.html
   http://www.plattsburgh.edu/legacy/global.htm
Workers' education: http://erols.com/czarlab/netlinks.html
IWW: http://www.iww.org
Left Business Observer: http://www.panix.com/~dhenwood/LBO_home.html
Hours of work: http://mindlink.net/knowware/worksite.htm

NOTES

INTRODUCTION

1. For good introductions to labor law, see Bruce Feldacker, *Labor Guide to Labor Law*, 3rd ed. (Englewood Cliffs, N.J.: Prentice-Hall, 1990) and David P. Twomey, *Labor and Employment Law*, 9th ed. (Cincinnati: South-Western Publishing Company, 1994).
2. An excellent critical examination of teams can be found in Mike Parker and Jane Slaughter, *Working Smart: A Union Guide to Participation Programs and Reengineering* (Detroit: Labor Education and Research Project, 1994).
3. Frank Elkouri and Edna A. Elkouri, *How Arbitration Works*, 5th ed. (Washington, D.C.: Bureau of National Affairs, 1997).
4. Lawrence Mishel, Jared Bernstein, and John Schmitt, *The State of Working America, 1996-97* (Armonk, N.Y.: M. E. Sharpe, 1997), chap. 5.
5. Michael D. Yates, *Longer Hours, Fewer Jobs: Employment and Unemployment in the United States* (New York: Monthly Review Press, 1994), chap. 4.
6. Lawrence and Ruy Texeira, *The Myth of the Coming Labor Shortage: Jobs, Skills, and Incomes of America's Workforce 2000* (Washington, D.C.: Economic Policy Institute, 1991) and Mishel, Bernstein, and Schmitt, *The State of Working America.*

CHAPTER ONE: WHY UNIONS?

1. Michael D. Yates, *Longer Hours, Fewer Jobs: Employment and Unemployment in the United States* (New York: Monthly Review Press, 1994), chap. 6.
2. Joan Roemer, *Two to Four from Nine to Five: The Adventures of a Daycare Provider* (New York: Harper & Row, 1989); Alison Clarke-Stewart, *Daycare* (Cambridge, Mass.: Harvard University Press, 1993).

3. On this tendency of workers to form unions, see, among many others, Sidney and Beatrice Webb, *The History of Trade Unionism* (Clifton, N.J.: Augustus M. Kelley, 1970); John R. Commons, *History of Labor in the United States*, 4 vols. (New York: Macmillan, 1918-1935); Selig Perlman, *The Theory of the Labor Movement* (New York: Augustus M. Kelley, 1973); A. Lozovsky, *Marx and the Trade Unions* (New York: International Publishers, 1942); John Anthony Moses, *Trade Union Theory from Marx to Walesa* (New York: Berg, 1990).

4. For examples of how formal groups form out of more spontaneous actions, see the essays in John Anner, ed., *Beyond Identity Politics* (Boston: South End Press, 1996).

5. Again, among many others, see Commons, *History of Labor in the United States*; Philip S. Foner, *History of the Labor Movement in the United States*, 9 vols. (New York: International Publishers, 1947-91); American Social History Project, *Who Built America?*, 2 vols. (New York: Pantheon Books, 1989-1992).

6. American Social History Project, *Who Built America?*, 1: 337.

7. The Philadelphia cordwainers were prosecuted and convicted of criminal "conspiracy" in the first famous labor law case in the United States. The case is *Commonwealth v Pullis,* cited in John R. Commons, et al., *Documentary History of the United States* (New York: Russell & Russell, 1958). See also William E. Forbath, *Law and the Shaping of the American Labor Movement* (Cambridge, Mass.: Harvard University Press, 1991).

8. American Social History Project, *Who Built America?* 1: 336.

9. The American Federation of Labor was founded by skilled craftsmen in 1886. See Philip S. Foner, *History of the Labor Movement in the United States,* vol. 2: *From the Founding of the AFL to the Emergence of American Imperialism* (New York: International Publishers, 1955).

10. Cafe Tartuffo, Inc., 261 NLRB 281 (1982). For other relevant legal material, see Michael D. Yates, *Power on the Job: The Legal Rights of Working People* (Boston: South End Press, 1994), chap. 4. For information on reading legal citations, see ibid., 279-81.

11. See the classic account of labor violence, Louis Adamic, *Dynamite: The Story of Class Violence in America* (1931; reprint New York: Chelsea House Publishers, 1968).

12. William J. Puette, *Through Jaundiced Eyes: How the Media Views Organized Labor* (Ithaca, N.Y.: ILR Press, 1992); Tom Zaniello, *Working Stiffs, Union Maids, Reds, and Riffraff: An Organized Guide to Films about Labor* (Ithaca: ILR Press, 1996).

13. Edward S. Herman and Noam Chomsky, *The Political Economy of Human Rights*, 2 vols. (Boston: South End Press, 1979), and Noam Chomsky and Edward S. Herman, *Manufacturing Consent: The Political Economy of the Mass Media* (New York: Pantheon Books, 1988).

14. Lawrence Mishel, Jared Bernstein, and John Schmitt, *The State of Working America, 1996-97* (Armonk, N.Y.: M. E. Sharpe, 1997), 199.

15. Thomas A. Kochan and Harry C. Katz, *Collective Bargaining and Industrial Relations*, 2nd ed. (Homewood, Ill.: Richard D. Irwin, 1985), 338-40.

16. See Mishel, Bernstein, and Schmitt, *The State of Working America*, 198-203.

17. Barry T. Hirsch and David A. Macpherson, *Union Membership and Earnings Data Book: Compilations from the Current Population Survey*, 1996 ed. (Washington, D.C.: The Bureau of National Affairs, 1996), tables 4, 5, and 6.

18. See, for example, Andreas Jorgenson, "Efficiency and Welfare Under Capitalism: *Denmark v The United States;* A Short Comparison," *Monthly Review* 48 (February 1997): 34-42.

19. On conditions in the early auto factories, see Sidney Fine, *Sit-Down: The General Motors Strike of 1936-37* (Ann Arbor: University of Michigan Press, 1969).

20. See the interesting films, *Taylor Chain, Part One*, 33 min., New Day Films, Hohokus, N.J., 1980, videocassette; and *Taylor Chain, Part Two*, 33 min., New Day Films, 1984, videocassette. It is in *Part Two* that one of the workers mentioned the whistling.

21. Richard B. Freeman and James L. Medoff, *What Do Unions Do?* (New York: Basic Books, 1984), 94-110.

CHAPTER TWO: HOW UNIONS FORM

1. William Forbath, "The Shaping of the American Labor Movement," *Harvard Law Review* 102 (January 1987): appendix B.

2. See the following books by a great labor historian, David Montgomery: *Beyond Equality: Labor and the Radical Republicans, 1862-1872* (New York: Knopf, 1967); *The Fall of the House of Labor: The Workplace, the State, and American Labor Activism, 1865-1925* (New York: Cambridge University Press, 1987); and *Citizen Worker: The Experience of Workers in the United States with Democracy and the Free Market during the Nineteenth Century* (New York: Cambridge University Press, 1993).

3. Haggai Hurvitz, "American Labor Law and the Doctrine of Entrepreneurial Property rights: Boycotts, Courts, and the Juridical Reorientation of 1886-1895," *Industrial Relations Law Journal* 8 (1986): 307-61.

4. Melvyn Dubofsky and Warren Van Tine, *John L. Lewis* (New York: Quadrangle/The New York Times Book Co., 1977); Herbert G. Gutman, "The Negro and the United Mine Workers of America: The Career and Letters of Richard L. Davis and Something of Their Meaning," in Julius Jacobson, ed., *The Negro and the American Labor Movement* (Garden City, N.J.: Anchor Books, 1968); American Social History Project, *Who Built America?* (New York: Pantheon Books, 1989-1992) 75-77.

5. Michael Rogin, "Volunteerism: The Political Functions of an Anti-Political Doctrine," *Industrial and Labor Relations Review* 15 (July 1962): 521-35.

6. "The Great Uprising" and many other labor revolts are described in Jeremy Brecher, *Strike* (Boston: South End Press, 1972). See also Philip S. Foner, *The Great Labor Uprising of 1877* (New York: Monad Press, 1977).

7. Brecher, *Strike;* Adamic, *Dynamite;* Paul Avrich, *The Haymarket Tragedy* (Princeton, N.J.: Princeton University Press, 1984).

8. Paul Krause, *The Battle for Homestead, 1880-1892: Politics, Culture, and Steel* (Pittsburgh: University of Pittsburgh Press, 1992).

9. Brecher, *Strike;* Rev. William H. Carwardine, *The Pullman Strike* (Chicago: Charles H. Kerr, 1973); Nick Salvatore, *Eugene V. Debs: Citizen and Socialist* (Urbana: University of Illinois Press, 1982).

10. Foner, *History of the Labor Movement in the United States,* vol. 8: *Post-War Struggles, 1918-1919* (New York: International Publishers, 1988), xi.

11. A good introduction to labor struggles in the Depression years is Irving Bernstein, *Turbulent Years: A History of the American Worker, 1933-1941* (Boston: Houghton Mifflin, 1969).

12. Read the interesting books by Farrell Dobbs: *Teamster Rebellion* (New York: Monad Press, 1972) and *Teamster Bureaucracy* (New York: Monad Press, 1977).

13. Michael Goldfield, *The Color of Politics* (New York: The New Press, 1997).

14. Michael T. Yates, *Power on the Job: The Legal Rights of Working People* (Boston: South End Press, 1994); Charles O. Gregory and Harold A. Katz, *Labor and the Law* (New York: W. W. Norton, 1979).

15. Yates, *Power on the Job,* chaps. 4, 5, and 6.

16. For the inside story, check out the book by former union buster, Martin J. Levitt, *Confessions of a Union Buster* (New York: Crown Publishers, 1993).

17. Kate Bronfenbrenner, "Organizing in the NAFTA Environment: How Companies Use 'Free Trade' to Stop Unions," *New Labor Forum* no. 1 (Fall 1997): 50-60.

18. Fernando Gapasin and Michael Yates, "Organizing the Unorganized: Will Promises Become Practices?," *Monthly Review* 49 (July-August 1997): 46-62.

19. Kate Bronfenbrenner and Tom Juravich, "The Impact of Employer Opposition on Union Certification Win Rates: A Private/Public Comparison," working paper no. 113, Economic Policy Institute, February 1995.

20. Joe Crump, "The Pressure's On: Organizing Without the NLRB," *Labor Research Review* no. 18: 33. See also "Labor's Corporate Campaign," *Labor Research Review* no. 21 (Fall/ Winter 1993).

21. Ashley Adams, "Winning Union Recognition Without the NLRB," *Labor Notes,* February 1993: 12.

22. Kate Bronfenbrenner and Tom Juravich, "Union Tactics Matter: The Impact of Union Tactics on Certification Elections, First contracts, and Membership Rates," working paper, Institute for the Study of Labor Organizations, no date.

23. Cited in Gapasin and Yates, "Organizing the Unorganized": 53.

24. Ibid.

25. Yates, *Power on the Job,* 7-11; Toni Gilpin et al., *On Strike for Respect: The Clerical and Technical Workers' Strike at Yale University* (Chicago: Charles H. Kerr, 1988).

26. A union can negotiate a "union shop" in which all members of the bargaining unit must become members of the union within a certain number of days. However, if a member of the unit challenges this, all that the union can do is force this person to become a "financial core" member, paying to the union a dues equivalent but not actually becoming a member. See Yates, *Power on the Job,* 136-37, and the legal cases cited therein.

CHAPTER THREE: UNION STRUCTURES AND DEMOCRACY

1. For example, a recent poll conducted by the United Food and Commercial Workers Union revealed among members "extreme disrespect and hostility toward the international union leadership" and "universal demoralization throughout the UFCW." This is cited in Association for Union Democracy, "How Do You Feel About the UFCW? Don't Ask!," *50+ Club News* 56 (June 1997): 8-9.

2. Farrell Dobbs, *Teamster Rebellion* (New York: Monad Press, 1972).

3. Steven Brill, *The Teamsters* (New York: Simon & Schuster, 1978); Kenneth C. Crowe, *Collision: How the Rank and File Took Back the Teamsters* (New York: Charles Scribner's Sons, 1993); and Dan La Botz, *Rank-and-File Rebellion: Teamsters for a Democratic Union* (London: Verso, 1990).

4. Bureau of National Affairs, *Directory of U. S. Labor Organizations* (Washington, D. C.: Bureau of National Affairs, 1997).

5. E. Edward Herman, *Collective Bargaining and Labor Relations*, 4th ed. (Upper Saddle River, N.J.: Prentice Hall, 1997), 75-92.

6. For an account of the Landrum-Griffin Act's provisions, see Yates, *Power on the Job*, chap. 7; Bruce Feldacker, *Labor Guide to Labor Law*, 3rd ed. (Englewood Cliffs, N.J.: Prentice Hall, 1990), chap. 11; H. W. Benson, *Democratic Rights for Union Members* (New York: Association for Union Democracy, 1979).

7. Paul F. Clark, *The Miners' Fight for Democracy: Arnold Miller and the Reform of the United Mine Workers* (Ithaca, N.Y.: ILR Press, 1981).

8. For a brief description of the overall structure of the AFL-CIO, see Arthur A. Sloane and Fred Witney, *Labor Relations*, 4th ed. (Englewood Cliffs, NJ: Prentice Hall, 1981).

9. Gapasin and Yates, "Organizing the Unorganized," 55-57.

10. On the UE, see Ronald W. Schatz, *The Electrical Workers: A History of Labor at General Electric and Westinghouse, 1923-60* (Urbana: University Of Illinois Press, 1983); and Ronald L. Filipelli and Mark D. McColloch, *Cold War in the Working Class: The Rise and Decline of the United Electrical Workers* (Albany: State University of New York Press, 1994). Much of this section is based upon the contents of various UE constitutions. I am grateful to UE District Council 6 for giving me copies of these.

11. For a good summary of the role of Communist Party activiss in the labor movement, see Roger Keeran, "The Communist Influence on American Labor," in Michael E. Brown, et al., eds., *New Studies in the Politics and Culture of U.S. Communism* (New York: Monthly Review Press, 1993), 163-98.

12. Michael Goldfield argues persuasively that the poor choices made by organized labor were important to the outcome of the attempt to organize the South after the Second World War. See "Race and the CIO: The Possibilities for Racial Egalitarianism During the 1930s and 1940s," *International Labor and Working-Class History* no. 44 (Fall 1993): 1-32; "Race and the CIO: Reply to Critics," *International Labor and Working-Class History* no. 46 (Fall 1994): 142-60; and "The Failure of Operation Dixie: A Critical Turning Point in American Political Development?," in *Race, Class, and Community in Southern Labor History*, eds. Gary M. Fink and Merl E. Reed (Tuscaloosa: University of Alabama Press, 1994), 166-88.

13. The quotes are taken from the UE constitutions.

14. See the following articles by Judith Stepan-Norris and Maurice Zeitlin: "'Red' Unions and 'Bourgeois' Contracts?," *American Journal of Sociology* 96 (1991): 1151-1200; "Union Democracy, Radical Leadership, and the

Hegemony of Capital," *American Sociological Review* 60 (December 1995): 829-50; "Insurgency, Radicalism, and Democracy in America's Industrial Unions," *Social Forces* 75 (September 1996): 1-32.

CHAPTER FOUR: COLLECTIVE BARGAINING

1. The legal duties of the parties to bargain collectively are spelled out in Sections 8(a)(5), 8(b)(3), and 9(a) of the National Labor Relations Act.
2. On the legal aspects of collective bargaining, see Michael T. Yates, *Power on the Job: The Legal Rights of Working People* (Boston: South End Press, 1994), chap. 5, and Bruce Feldacker, *Labor Guide to Labor Law*, 3rd ed. (Englewood Cliffs, N.J.: Prentice Hall, 1990), chap. 5.
3. U.S. Department of Labor, *Fact Finding Report: Commission on the Future of Worker-Management Relations* (Washington, D.C.: Government Printing Office, May 1994), 81-87.
4. Kate Bronfenbrenner and Tom Juravich, "The Impact of Employer Opposition on Union Certification Win Rates: A Private/Public Comparison," working paper no. 113, Economic Policy Institute, February 1995; Bronfenbrenner and Juravich, "Union Tactics Matter: The Impact of Union Tactics on Certification Elections, First contracts, and Membership Rates," working paper, Institute for the Study of Labor Organizations, no date; Bronfenbrenner, "Organizing in the NAFTA Environment: How Companies Use 'Free Trade' to Stop Unions," *New Labor Forum* no. 1 (Fall 1997): 50-60.
5. Many books and articles have been written on the IWW. A good starting point is Melvyn Dubofsky, *We Shall Be All: A History of the IWW* (New York: Quadrangle/The New York Times Book Co., 1969).
6. Rick Hurd, "New Deal Labor Policy and the Containment of Radical Union Activity," *The Review of Radical Political Economics* 8 (Fall 1976), 32-44.
7. Paul F. Clark, Peter Gottlieb, and Donald Kennedy, eds., *Forging a Union in Steel: Philip Murray, SWOC, and the United Steelworkers* (Ithaca, N.Y.: ILR Press, 1987).
8. Kim Moody, *An Injury to All: The Decline of American Unionism* (New York: Verso, 1988).
9. "UAW Steamrolled," *Multinational Monitor* 16 (December 1995): 5; Tom Johnson, "Caterpillar Bulldozed the United Auto Workers," *Business and Society Review,* Winter 1990: 38; Peter Elstrom, "This Cat Keeps on Purring: Caterpillar's Plan is Paying Off," *Business Week,* 20 January 1997: 82.
10. Service Employees International Union, *Contract Campaign Manual* (Washington, D.C.: Service Employees International Union, 1988).

11. The Bureau of National Affairs, *1997 Source Book on Collective Bargaining: Wages, Benefits, and Other Contract Issues* (Washington, D.C.: The Bureau of National Affairs, 1997).

12. Yates, *Power on the Job*, chap. 5; Feldacker, *Labor Guide to Labor Law*, chap. 5; Robert M. Schwartz, *The Legal Rights of Union Stewards*, 2nd ed. (Cambridge, Mass.: Work Rights Press, 1994), chap. 4.

13. Service Employees International Union, *Contract Campaign Manual*, parts 2 and 4.

14. For a good description of a corporate campaign, see Peter Rachleff, *Hard-Pressed in the Heartland: The Hormel Strike and the Future of the Labor Movement* (Boston: South End Press, 1993). See also "Labor's Corporate Campaigns," *Labor Research Review* no. 21 (Fall/Winter 1993).

15. Thomas A. Kochan and Harry C. Katz, *Collective Bargaining and Industrial Relations*, 2nd ed. (Homewood, Ill.: Richard D. Irwin, 1985), 102-48.

16. See Sam Gindin, *Canadian Auto Workers: the Birth and Transformation of a Union* (Toronto: James Lorimer, 1995).

17. See Philip S. Foner, *U.S. Labor and the Vietnam War* (New York: International Publishers, 1989), 1-8.

18. On this and on the repression of labor generally, see Robert Justin Goldstein, *Political Repression in Modern America* (New York: Schenkman Publishing Co., Inc., 1978). On Haywood's escape to Russia, see Dubofsky, *We Shall Be All*, 459-61.

19. American Social History Project, *Who Built America?* vol. 2 (New York: Pantheon Books, 1992), 461-63.

20. An interesting reference on this period is Ann Fagen Ginger and David Christiano, eds., *The Cold War Against Labor*, 2 vols. (Berkeley, Calif.: Meiklejohn Civil Liberties Institute, 1987). See also Steve Rosswurm, ed., *The CIO's Left-Led Unions* (New Brunswick, N.J.: Rutgers University Press, 1992).

21. For a good summary of this position, as well as the alternative view, see Victor G. Devinatz, "An Alternative Strategy: Lessons from the UAW Local 6 and the FE, 1946-52," in Cyrus Bina, Laurie Clements, and Chuck Davis, eds., *Beyond Survival: Wage Labor in the Late Twentieth Century* (Armonk, N.Y.: M. E. Sharpe, 1996), 145-60.

22. Interesting, useful, and accessible to nonspecialists are William Ury and Roger Fisher, *Getting to Yes: Negotiating Agreement Without Giving In* (Boston: Houghton Mifflin, 1981) and William Ury, *Getting Past No: Negotiating Your Way From Confrontation to Cooperation* (New York: Bantam Books, 1993).

23. Ury, *Getting Past No,* 31-51.

24. Ibid., pp. 21-26.

25. The negotiations described in the text can be seen in a remarkable video, *Final Offer,* 78 min., California Newsreel, 1985, videocassette.

26. Ury and Fisher, *Getting To Yes,* chap. 5.

27. Feldacker, *Labor Guide to Labor Law,* 147-48.

28. Ellen Dannin, "Legislative Intent and Impasse Resolution Under the National Labor Relations Act: Does It Matter?," *Hofstra Labor & Employment Law Journal* 15 (Fall 1997): 11-43.

29. Michael D. Yates, "From the Coal Wars to the Pittston Strike," *Monthly Review* 42 (June 1990): 25-39.

30. Max H. Bazeman, "The General Basis of Arbitrator Behavior: An Empirical Analysis of Conventional and Final-Offer Arbitration," *Econometrica* 54 (July 1986): 819-44; Orley Ashenfelter and David Bloom, "Models of Arbitration Behavior: Theory and Evidence," *American Economic Review* 74 (March 1984): 111-24.

31. Edwin F. Beal, Edward D. Wickersham, and Philip K. Kienast, *The Practice of Collective Bargaining,* 5th ed. (Homewood, Ill.: Richard D. Irwin, 1976), chaps. 9-13.

32. Staughton Lynd, *Solidarity Unionism* (Chicago: Charles H. Kerr, 1992).

33. Bureau of National Affairs, *Basic Patterns in Union Contracts,* 14th ed. (Washington, D.C.: Bureau of National Affairs, 1995), 34. This source states that 98 percent of all agreements have arbitration clauses. Since the courts generally consider, as does management, that a no-strike clause is the *quid pro quo* for the arbitration clause, it is safe to say that nearly all contracts have explicit or implied no-strike agreements.

34. Feldacker, *Labor Guide to Labor Law,* 199-201.

35. Mike Parker and Jane Slaughter, *Working Smart: A Union Guide to Participation Programs and Reengineering* (Detroit: Labor Education and Research Project, 1994).

36. William DiFazio, *Longshoremen: Community and Resistance on the Brooklyn Waterfront* (Hedley, Mass.: Bergin and Garvey, 1985).

37. David W. Ewing, *Justice on the Job: Resolving Grievances in the Nonunion Workplace* (Boston: Harvard Business School Press, 1989).

38. Gertrude Ezorsky, *Racism and Justice: The Case for Affirmative Action* (Ithaca, N.Y.: ILR Press, 1991); Steven Briggs, "Allocating Available Work in a Union Environment: Seniority vs. Work Sharing," *Labor Law Journal* 38 (October 1987): 650-57; Michele M. Hoyman, "Alternative Models of Compliance by Unions with Civil Rights Legislation," *Law & Policy* 8

(January 1986): 77-103; Casey Ichniowski, "Have Angels Done More?: The Steel Industry Consent Decree," *Industrial and Labor Relations Review* 36 (January 1983): 182-98.

39. Schwartz, *The Legal Rights of Shop Stewards,* chap. 4.
40. Frank Elkouri and Edna A. Elkouri, *How Arbitration Works,* 5th ed. (Washington, D.C.: BNA Books, 1997).
41. Yates, *Power on the Job,* chap. 7.
42. Devinatz, "An Alternative Strategy."
43. Judith Stepan-Norris and Maurice Zeitlin, "'Red' Unions and 'Bourgeois' Contracts?," *American Journal of Sociology* 96 (1991): 1151-1200; "Union Democracy, Radical Leadership, and the Hegemony of Capital," *American Sociological Review* 60 (December 1995): 829-850; "Insurgency, Radicalism, and Democracy in America's Industrial Unions," *Social Forces* 75 (September 1996): 1-32.

CHAPTER FIVE: UNIONS AND POLITICS

1. Michael D. Yates, *Longer Hours, Fewer Jobs: Employment and Unemployment in the United States* (New York: Monthly Review Press, 1994), chap. 5.
2. Don J. Lofgren, *Dangerous Premises: An Insider's View of OSHA Enforcement* (Ithaca, N.Y.: ILR Press, 1989).
3. Michael D. Yates, *Labor Law Handbook* (Boston: South End Press, 1987), 77-79; *Workplace Health and Safety: A Guide to Collective Bargaining* (Berkeley, Calif.: Labor Occupational Health Program, 1980).
4. Lawrence Mishel, Jared Bernstein, and John Schmitt, *The State of Working America, 1996-97* (Armonk, N.Y.: M. E. Sharpe, 1997), 156-61. It was estimated that "More than a fifth of all African-Americans and 38 percent of all Mexican-Americans lacked health insurance in 1992, compared with 18 percent of Puerto Ricans and 16 percent of whites." There have been no dramatic improvements since then. Nancy Folbre and the Center for Popular Economics, *The New Field Guide to the U.S. Economy* (New York: The New Press, 1995), 7.12.
5. Richard B. Freemen, "Unionism Comes to the Public Sector," *Journal of Economic Literature* 24 (March 1986): 41-86.
6. Among many others, see these books by G. William Domhoff: *Who Rules America?* (Englewood Cliffs, N.J.: Prentice Hall, 1967); *The Higher Circles: The Governing Class in America* (New York: Random House, 1970); *The Power Elite and the State: How Policy is Made in America* (New York: A. de Gruyter, 1990).

7. William Forbath, "The Shaping of the American Labor Movement," *Harvard Law Review* 102 (January 1987).

8. Wolfgang Abendroth, *A Short History of the European Working Class* (New York: Monthly Review Press, 1972).

9. Isaiah Berlin, *Karl Marx: His Life and Environment* (New York: Oxford University Press, 1996).

10. Selig Perlman, *The Theory of the Labor Movement* (New York: Augustus M. Kelley, 1973); Mark Perlman, *Labor Union Theories in America: Background and Development* (Evanston, Ill.: Row Peterson, 1958); James Weinstein, *The Decline of Socialism in America, 1912-1925* (New York: Monthly Review Press, 1967); David Milton, *The Politics of U. S. Labor: From the Great Depression to the New Deal* (New York: Monthly Review Press, 1982); Mike Davis, *Prisoners of the American Dream: Politics and Economy in the History of the U. S. Working Class* (London: Verso, 1986).

11. David Montgomery, *Citizen Worker: The Experience of Workers in the United States with Democracy and the Free Market during the Nineteenth Century* (New York: Cambridge University Press, 1993); Christopher L. Tomlins, *Law, Labor and Ideology in the Early American Republic* (New York: Cambridge University Press, 1993).

12. David R. Roediger, *The Wages of Whiteness: Race and the Making of the American Working Class* (London: Verso, 1991); Philip S. Foner, *Organized Labor and the Black Worker: 1619-1973* (New York: Praeger, 1974).

13. Seymour Martin Lipset, *Continental Divide: The Values and Institutions of the United States and Canada* (New York: Routledge, 1990); Seymour Martin Lipset, *The First New Nation: The United States in Historical and Comparative Perspective* (New York: Basic Books, 1963).

14. Robert Justin Goldstein, *Political Repression in Modern America* (New York: Schenkman Publishing Co., Inc., 1978).

15. American Social History Project, *Who Built America?*, vol. 2 (New York: Pantheon Books, 1992), 144-52, 184-88; Philip S. Foner, *History of the Labor Movement in the United States*, vols. 3 and 4 (New York: International Publishers, 1964, 1965); Samuel Gompers, *Seventy Years of Life and Labor: An Autobiography* (Ithaca, N.Y.: ILR Press, 1984).

16. Michael Rogin, "Volunteerism: The Political Functions of an Anti-Political Doctrine," *Industrial and Labor Relations Review* 15 (July 1962).

17. There have been numerous Congressional hearings and commissions concerning labor racketeering. See, for example, President's Commission on Organized Crime, *The Edge: Organized Crime, Business, and Labor Unions* (Washington, D.C.: Government Printing Office, 1986). See also

Philip Taft, *Corruption and Racketeering in the Labor Movement* (Ithaca, N.Y.: New York State School of Industrial and Labor Relations, 1970).

18. Milton, *The Politics of U.S. Labor.*
19. Ibid.; Melvyn Dubofsky and Warren Van Tine, *John L. Lewis* (New York: Quadrangle/The New York Times Book Co., 1977).
20. Kim Moody, *An Injury to All: The Decline of American Unionism* (New York: Verso, 1988).
21. Arthur A. Sloane and Fred Witney, *Labor Relations*, 4th ed. (Englewood Cliffs, N.J.: Prentice Hall, 1981), chap. 4.
22. For example, see the recent AFL-CIO booklet, *America Needs a Raise* (Washington, D.C.: AFL-CIO Department of Economic Research, 1996).
23. Ibid., 21-24.
24. Ibid., 24-28.
25. Yates, *Labor Law Handbook*, chap. 6.
26. Such jobs were featured in Tony Horowitz, "9 to Nowhere," *Wall Street Journal,* 1 December 1994: A1.
27. David Card and Alan B. Krueger, *Myth and Measurement: The New Economics of the Minimum Wage* (Princeton, N.J.: Princeton University Press, 1995).
28. U.S. House of Representatives Committee on Government Operations, *High Skills, Low Wages: Productivity and the False Promise of NAFTA* (Washington, D.C.: Government Printing Office, 1993); Ricardo Grinspun and Maxwell Cameron, eds., *The Political Economy of Free Trade* (New York: St. Martin's Press, 1993).
29. Sarah Anderson and Ken Silverstein, "All the President's Handouts," *Harper's* 288 (March 1994): 21-23.
30. Robert B. Reich, *Locked in the Cabinet* (New York: Alfred A. Knopf, 1997).
31. Michael D. Yates, "Does the U.S. Labor Movement Have a Future?," *Monthly Review* 48, no. 9 (February 1997).
32. Bertram Gross, *Friendly Fascism: The New Face of Power in America* (Boston: South End Press, 1980).
33. Taken from Yates, *Labor Law Handbook*, chap. 6.
34. David Ellwood and Glenn Fine, "The Impact of Right-to-Work Laws on Union Organizing," *Journal of Political Economy* 95 (April 1987): 250-73.
35. See Foner, *History of the Labor Movement in the United States,* vols. 2 through 5; Foner, *U.S. Labor and the Vietnam War* (New York: International Publishers, 1989); Ronald Radosh, *American Labor and United States Foreign Policy* (New York: Random House, 1969).
36. The AFL actually helped the government in its war against the radical unions. See Goldstein, *Political Repression,* 124.

37. Gabriel Kolko, *The Roots of American Foreign Policy: An Analysis of Power and Purpose* (Boston: Beacon Press, 1969); John Lewis Gaddis, *The United States and the Origins of the Cold War, 1941-1947* (New York: Columbia University Press, 1972); Marty Jezer, *The Dark Ages: Life in the United States, 1945-1960* (Boston: South End Press, 1982).

38. Edward S. Herman and Noam Chomsky, *The Political Economy of Human Rights*, 2 vols. (Boston: South End Press, 1979); Jenny Pearce, *Under the Eagle: U. S. Intervention in Central America and the Caribbean* (Boston: South End Press, 1982).

39. Stephan Slesinger and Stephen Kinzer, *Bitter Fruit: The Untold Story of the American Coup in Guatemala* (Garden City, N.J.: Doubleday, 1982).

40. Jenny Pearce, *Promised Land: Peasant Rebellion in Chalatenango, El Salvador* (London: Latin America Bureau, 1986).

41. Carlos Vilas, *The Sandinista Revolution: National Liberation and Social Transformation* (New York: Monthly Review Press, 1986).

CHAPTER SIX: UNIONS, RACISM, AND SEXISM

1. Peter Meiksens, "Same as It Ever Was?: The Structure of the Working Class," *Monthly Review* 49 (July-August 1997): 31-45; Harry Braverman, *Labor and Monopoly Capital: The Degradation of Labor in the Twentieth Century* (New York: Monthly Review Press, 1974).

2. Roger Horowitz, *"Negro and White, Unite and Fight": A Social History of Industrial Unionism in Meatpacking, 1930-90* (Urbana and Chicago: University of Illinois Press, 1997).

3. Teresa Amott and Julie Matthaei, *Race, Gender, and Work: A Multi-Cultural Economic History of Women in the United States* (Boston: South End Press, 1996).

4. American Social History Project, *Who Built America?*, vol. 2 (New York: Pantheon Books, 1992), 167-84.

5. Philip S. Foner, *Organized Labor and the Black Worker: 1619-1973* (New York: Praeger, 1974); Eric Foner, *Nothing But Freedom: Emancipation and Its Legacy* (Baton Rouge: Louisiana State University Press, 1983); Robin D. G. Kelley, *Race Rebels: Culture, Politics, and the Black Working Class* (New York: The Free Press, 1996).

6. Warren Whatley, "African-American Strikebreaking from the Civil War to the New Deal," *Social Science History* 17 (Winter 1993): 525-58.

7. Amott and Matthaei, *Race, Gender, and Work*. For detailed data on the labor force, wages, and other worker characteristics, see the January issues of the Department of Labor publication, *Employment and Earnings*. For

historical data, see United States Bureau of the Census, *Historical Statistics of the United States, Colonial Times to 1970* (Washington, D.C.: Government Printing Office, 1975).

8. Ronald G. Ehrenberg and Robert S. Smith, *Modern Labor Economics: Theory and Public Policy,* 6th ed. (Reading, Mass.: Addison-Wesley, 1997), 654.
9. Randy E. Ilg, "The Changing Face of Farm Employment," *Monthly Labor Review* 118 (April 1995): 8; Mary C. King, "Occupational Segregation By Race and Sex, 1940-88," *Monthly Labor Review* 115 (April 1992): 31.
10. See, for example, Lynn C. Burbridge, "The Reliance of African-American Women on Government and Third-Sector Employment," *The American Economic Review* 84 (May 1994): 103-107.
11. Ehrenberg and Smith, *Modern Labor Economics,* 414.
12. Barry T. Hirsch and David A. Macpherson, *Union Membership and Earnings Data Book: Compilations from the Current Population Survey,* 1996 ed. (Washington, D.C.: The Bureau of National Affairs, 1996), 19.
13. See Michael Yates, "Organizing African Americans: Some Economic and Legal Dimensions" (paper presented at the conference on "African Americans, Labor, and Society: Organizing for A New Agenda," Wayne State University, Detroit, Michigan, June 1996).
14. Michael Goldfield, "Race and Labor Organization in the United States," *Monthly Review* 49 (July-August 1997): 80-97.
15. Eric Arnesen, *Waterfront Workers of New Orleans: Race, Class, and Politics, 1893-1923* (New York: Oxford University Press, 1991).
16. Amott and Matthaei, *Race, Gender, and Work.*
17. Roger Keeran, "The Communist Influence on American Labor," in Michael E. Brown, et al., eds., *New Studies in the Politics and Culture of U. S. Communism* (New York: Monthly Review Press, 1993); Steve Rosswurm, ed., *The CIO's Left-Led Unions* (New Brunswick, N.J.: Rutgers University Press, 1992); Bert Cochran, *Labor and Communism: The Conflict That Shaped American Unions* (Princeton, N.J.: Princeton University Press, 1977).
18. Herbert G. Gutman, "The Negro and the United Mine Workers of America: The Career and Letters of Richard L. Davis and Something of Their Meaning," in Julius Jacobson, ed., *The Negro and the American Labor Movement* (Garden City, N.J.: Anchor Books, 1968); John William Trotter, *Coal, Class, and Color: Blacks in Southern West Virginia* (Urbana: University of Illinois Press, 1990).
19. Cited in Michael Goldfield, "Race and the CIO: Reply to Critics," *International Labor and Working-Class History* no. 46 (Fall 1994): 2.

20. Ibid.: 20-21; Bruce Nelson, "Class and Race in the Crescent City: The ILWU From San Francisco to New Orleans," in *The CIO's Left-Led Unions*, ed. Rosswurm, 19-46.

21. On this issue, see the fine documentary film by Tony Buba, *Struggles in Steel*, 58 min., California Newsreel, 1996, videocassette.

22. Taken from Horowitz, *"Negro and White, Unite and Fight."*

23. Ibid., 223.

24. On the porters, see William H. Harris, *Keeping the Faith: A. Philip Randolph, Milton P. Webster, and the Brotherhood of Sleeping Car Porters, 1925-37* (Urbana: University of Illinois Press, 1977). On the farmworkers, see Sam Kushner, *The Long Road to Delano* (New York: International Publishers, 1975).

25. David Bacon, "Face-Off in Watsonville: Strawberry Workers Pick Sides," *The Progressive* 61 (August 1997): 21-23.

26. For an excellent introduction, see Barbara Mayer Wertheimer, *We Were There: The Story of Working Women in America* (New York: Pantheon Books, 1977).

27. This table is based on one from Dorothy Sue Cobble, "Remaking Unions for the New Majority," in *Women and Unions: Forging a Partnership*, ed. Dorothy Sue Cobble (Ithaca, N.Y.: ILR Press, 1993), p. 11. The Coalition of Labor Union women (CLUW) kindly provided me with updated numbers, as collected by CLUW intern Silke Roth.

28. Horowitz, *"Negro and White, Unite and Fight,"* 227-42.

29. Mishel, Bernstein, and Schmitt, *The State of Working America*, 79-94.

30. Susan Cowell, "Family Policy: A Union Approach," in Cobble, ed., *Women and Unions*, 115-28; Carolyn York, "Bargaining for Work and Family Benefits," in ibid., 129-43. For another view, see Alice H. Cook, "Comments," in ibid., 148-56.

31. Mary Harris Jones, *The Autobiography of Mother Jones* (1925; reprint, ed. Mary Field Parton, Chicago: Illinois Labor History Society, 1972).

32. Tera Hunter, "Domination and Resistance: The Politics of Wage Household Labor in New South Atlanta," *Labor History* 34 (Spring-Summer 1993): 205-20.

33. Wertheimer, *We Were There*, 293-317.

34. Ibid., pp. 353-68; Ardis Cameron, *Radicals of the Worst Sort: Laboring Women in Lawrence, Massachusetts, 1860-1912* (Urbana: University of Illinois Press, 1993).

35. Vicki L. Ruiz, *Cannery Women, Cannery Lives: Mexican Women, Unionization, and the California Food Processing Industry, 1930-1950* (Albuquerque: University of New Mexico Press, 1987).

36. Amott and Matthaei, *Race, Gender, and Work*, 90.

37. Toni Gilpin et al., *On Strike for Respect: The Clerical and Technical Workers' Strike at Yale University* (Chicago: Charles H. Kerr, 1988).

38. These examples are drawn from Ruth Needleman, "Organizing Low-Wage Workers: Building for the Long Haul between Unions and Community-Based Organizations," *Working USA* 1 (May-June 1997): 45-59. Also, see Ellen Mayock Starbird, "Organizing in Home Health Care Work: Sexism, Poverty, and Racism," paper presented at the 92nd meeting of the American Sociological Association, Toronto, Canada, 9-13 August 1997.

39. Needleman, "Organizing Low-Wage Workers": 56.

40. Ibid.: 52-56.

41. Ibid.: 56.

42. Patti R. Roberts, "Comments," in Cobble, ed., *Women and Unions*, 349-56.

43. Cowell, "Family Policy," 117.

44. Michael Goldberg, "Affirmative Action in Union Government: The Landrum-Griffin Act implications," *Ohio State Law Journal* 44 (1983): 649-89; Elizabeth M. Iglesias, "Structures of Subordination: Women of Color at the Intersection of Title VII and the NLRA. Not!," *Harvard Civil Rights-Civil Liberties Law Review* 28 (1993): 395-503.

45. Fernando Gapasin, "Race, Gender and Other 'Problems' of Unity for the American Working Class," *Race, Gender & Class* 4, no. 1 (1996): 41-62.

46. Cowell, "Family Policy."

47. Ruth Milkman, "Organizing Immigrant Women in New York's Chinatown: An Interview with Katie Quan," in Cobble, ed., *Women and Unions*, 281-98.

48. Camille Colatosi and Elaine Karg, *Stopping Sexual Harassment* (Detroit: The Labor Education and Research Project, 1992).

49. "Collective Agreement Between The Ontario Public Service Employees Union and The Crown in Right of Ontario" (1992-1993), 30-32.

50. Herbert Hill, "Black Workers, Organized Labor, and Title VII of the 1964 Civil Rights Act: Legislative History and Litigation Record," in *Race in America: The Struggle for Equality*. eds. Herbert Hill and James E. Jones (Madison: University of Wisconsin Press, 1993), 263-344.

CHAPTER SEVEN: THE TASKS AHEAD

1. Richard B. Freeman and James L. Medoff, *What Do Unions Do?* (New York: Basic Books, 1984).

2. For the various density figures, see Hirsch and Macpherson, *Union Membership and Earnings Data Book.*

3. Bureau of National Affairs, "AFL-CIO Statistics on Paid Membership of Union Affiliates Prepared for Federation's 21st Constitutional Convention," 12 October 1995.

4. See Lisa Williamson, "Union Mergers: 1985-94 Update," *Monthly Labor Review* 118 (February 1995): 18-24.

5. Bureau of National Affairs, "AFL-CIO Statistics on Paid Membership."

6. Clara Chang and Constance Sorrentino, "Union Membership Statistics in 12 Countries," *Monthly Labor Review* 114 (December 1991): 46-53.

7. The statistic for New Zealand was provided by Ellen Dannin.

8. Kenneth C. Crowe, *Collision: How the Rank and File Took Back the Teamsters* (New York: Charles Scribner's Sons, 1993), 25-26.

9. Norman Eiger, "The Swedish Model: From the Cradle to the Grave?," in *Beyond Survival: Wage Labor in the Late Twentieth Century* (Armonk, N.Y.: M. E. Sharpe, 1996), eds. Cyrus Bina, Laurie Clements, and Chuck Davis, 87-108.

10. Isaac Shapiro and Marion Nichols, *Far from Fixed* (Washington, D.C.: Center on Budget and Policy Priorities, 1992).

11. Lawrence Mishel, Jared Bernstein, and John Schmitt, *The State of Working America, 1996-97* (Armonk, N.Y.: M. E. Sharpe, 1997), chap. 8.

12. This section relies heavily upon the following sources: Michael D. Yates, "Does the U.S. Labor Movement Have a Future?," *Monthly Review* 48, no. 9 (February 1997); Fernando Gapasin and Michael Yates, "Organizing the Unorganized: Will Promises Become Practices?," *Monthly Review* 49 (July-August 1997): 46-62; Kim Moody, *An Injury to All: The Decline of American Unionism* (New York: Verso, 1988); Bina, Clements, and Davis, eds., *Beyond Survival*; Doug Henwood, "Talking About Work," *Monthly Review* 49 (July-August 1997): 18-30; Jim Crotty and Gerald Epstein, "In Defense of Capital Controls," in *Are There Alternatives? Socialist Register 1996*, ed. Leo Panitch (London: Merlin Press, 1996), 118-49; Howard Botwinnick, *Persistent Inequalities* (Princeton, N.J.: Princeton University Press, 1994); Richard Freeman and Joel Rogers, "Worker Representation and Participation Survey: First Report of Findings," Proceedings of the 47th Annual Industrial Relations Research Association Meeting, 1994 (Madison, Wis.: Industrial Relations Research Association, 1995), 336-45; Center for Popular Economics, *Common Sense Economics* (Washington, D.C.: AFL-CIO, 1997); Michael Goldfield, *The Decline of Organized Labor in the United States* (Chicago: University of Chicago Press, 1987).

13. Michael D. Yates, *Power on the Job: The Legal Rights of Working People* (Boston: South End Press, 1994); Paul Weiler, "Promises to Keep: Securing

Workers' Rights to Self-Organization Under the NLRA," *Harvard Law Review* 102 (January 1989): 1111-1256.

14. Gapasin and Yates, "Organizing the Unorganized": 50-51.
15. David Bacon, "West Coast Janitors Get Ready to Fight," *Z Magazine* 10 (April 1997): 16-18; Paul Johnson, *Success While Others Fail* (Ithaca, N.Y.: Cornell University Press, 1994); Marc Cooper, "Labor Deals a New Hand," *The Nation* 264 (24 March 1997): 11-16.
16. This is one of the themes of Center for Popular Economics, *Common Sense Economics*, cited in note 12 above.
17. D. M. Kotz, T. McDonough, and M. Reich, *Social Structures of Accumulation: The Political Economy of Growth and Crisis* (New York: Cambridge University Press, 1994).
18. AFL-CIO Department of Economic Research, *America Needs a Raise*, 1.
19. Harry Braverman, *Labor and Monopoly Capital: The Degradation of Labor in the Twentieth Century* (New York: Monthly Review Press, 1974).
20. Moody, *An Injury to All.*
21. Paul F. Clark, *The Miners' Fight for Democracy: Arnold Miller and the Reform of the United Mine Workers* (Ithaca, N.Y.: ILR Press, 1981).
22. Kim Moody, "American Labor: A Movement Again?," *Monthly Review* 49 (July-August 1997): 63-79.
23. Robert Fitch, "America Needs a Raise," *The Nation* 263 (25 November 1996): 25-28.
24. Joseph C. Goulden, *Meany* (New York: Atheneum, 1972), 466-67.
25. Ben Hamper, *Rivethead* (New York: Warner Books, 1991).
26. Judith Stepan-Norris and Maurice Zeitlin, "'Red' Unions and 'Bourgeois' Contracts?," *American Journal of Sociology* 96 (1991): 1157-1159, and sources cited therein.
27. Ibid.; Judith Stepan-Norris and Maurice Zeitlin, "Union Democracy, Radical Leadership, and the Hegemony of Capital," *American Sociological Review* 60 (December 1995), and "Insurgency, Radicalism, and Democracy in America's Industrial Unions," *Social Forces* 75 (September 1996).
28. Michael Goldfield, "Race and the CIO: The Possibilities for Racial Egalitarianism During the 1930s and 1940s," *International Labor and Working-Class History* no. 44 (Fall 1993): 1-32; "Race and the CIO: Reply to Critics," *International Labor and Working-Class History* no. 46 (Fall 1994): 142-160; "The Failure of Operation Dixie: A Critical Turning Point in American Political Development?" in *Race, Class, and Community in Southern Labor History,* eds. Gary M. Fink and Merl E. Reed (Tuscaloosa: University of Alabama Press, 1994), 166-88.

29. Moody, "American Labor: A Movement Again?"
30. Cooper, "Labor Deals a New Hand": 12-14.
31. Ibid., 14.
32. Ibid.
33. Gapasin and Yates, "Organizing the Unorganized": 54-57.
34. Cooper, "Labor Deals a New Hand": 14.
35. David Bacon, "Evening the Odds: Cross-Border Organizing Gives Labor a Chance," *The Progressive* 61 (July 1997): 29-33.
36. Sumner M. Rosen, "Renewing Labor's Power and Vision," in *A World That Works: Building Blocks for a Just and Sustainable Society,* ed. Trent Schroyer (New York: The Bootstrap Press, 1997), 136-37.
37. Andrew Herod, "The Practice of International Labor Solidarity and the Geography of the Global Economy," *Economic Geography* 71 (October 1995): 341.
38. Kim Moody, *Labor in a Lean World: Unions in the International Economy* (New York: Verso, 1997).
39. Center for Popular Economics, *Common Sense Economics.*
40. Remarkably, many union contracts allow an employer to assign mandatory overtime. For good insights into the issue of shorter hours, see Juliet Schor, *The Overworked American: The Unexpected Decline of Leisure* (New York: Basic Books, 1991); David R. Roediger and Philip S. Foner, *Our Own Time: A History of American Labor and the Working Class* (London: Verso, 1989); Benjamin Hunnicut, *Work Without End: Abandoning Shorter Hours for the Right to Work* (Philadelphia: Temple University Press, 1989).

INDEX

7/99